THE ANCIENT SYNAGOGUES
OF THE IBERIAN PENINSULA
by Don A. Halperin

UNIVERSITY OF FLORIDA PRESS / GAINESVILLE, 1969

COPYRIGHT © 1969 BY THE BOARD OF
COMMISSIONERS OF STATE INSTITUTIONS
OF FLORIDA

LIBRARY OF CONGRESS
CATALOG CARD NO. 78-625777
SBN 8130-0272-9

PRINTED BY STORTER PRINTING COMPANY
GAINESVILLE, FLORIDA

PREFACE

This study makes an attempt to define the architectural forms used by the Jews in the religious structures they built on the Iberian Peninsula prior to 1506, the year of their exile from Portugal.

The writer traversed Spain and Portugal by automobile, in 1966 and again in 1968, visiting those sites which might possibly be fruitful. Among the many disappointments was the situation in Lorca: the last remains of the ancient synagogue there had been bulldozed in 1964. Elsewhere buildings proved to be inaccessible because they were locked and the keys were in the possession of someone many miles distant. However, enough buildings were photographed and measured for a distinguishable architectural pattern to present itself in plan, design, and structural form. A contrast became evident between the evolution of the ordinary synagogue with its many ancillary rooms and that of the great synagogue with perhaps only one auxiliary room for study and one more for legal procedures (or for housing students). It also became apparent that the well-documented ornamentation in carved plaster in the ordinary synagogues of Córdoba and Toledo's El Tránsito was unusual and reflected the desires of the individual donors of these fine buildings. More common was the plain stucco of Cáceres and Paredes de Nava; it has heretofore been believed that the latter was originally built as a church. In fact, the latest and possibly the most splendid synagogue ever built in Spain—now the Church of Mosen Rubi in Avila—exhibits great beauty in the stark simplicity of its stone walls. Until this writing, it has also been thought that this structure was first built as a Christian church.

There has been little effort at precise documentation in this monograph. Scholarship was not the objective of my searches or of this writing. The bibliography will adequately indicate my sources.

I am indebted to the American Philosophical Society, the Wolfson Family Foundation, and the University of Florida, whose grants helped finance the trips. Thanks are also due those with whom I had private conversations: Father Chamorro, a Jesuit student in the college at Oña; Father Latur, a Jesuit teacher in Tudela; the Reverend Borras, a Baptist minister in Barcelona; Dr. Amzalak, president of the Jewish Community of Lisbon; Professor Viegas Guerriero of the University of Lisbon; and Miss Pilar Mantilla of the tourist office in Avila. A great many thanks must go to Mrs. Lynda Kirkland who typed the text from my illegible scrawl. Finally, I am indebted to Professor Loys A. Johnson, chairman of the Department of Building Construction at the University of Florida, who arranged my teaching schedule so that I had time to write.

Unless otherwise marked, all photographs are by author.

Don A. Halperin

January, 1969

CONTENTS

99651

Location Map

1. HISTORY

It is reasonable to state that the Jews settled in the Iberian Peninsula at least 2,500 years ago, when the first Jerusalem temple fell, because at that time they scattered around the shores of the Mediterranean. Actually, Jews probably came to Spain even earlier as traders with the Phoenicians, who are known to have settled several coastal towns, such as Nazare, Benicarlo, and Elche, possibly as early as the eleventh century BCE.[1] It is possible that there were Jews with the Carthaginians when they conquered Barcelona in the third century BCE. Several authors feel that the Jews were the original settlers of Toledo and that perhaps the name *Toledo* itself is derived from the Hebrew *toledoth* which means "generations." (Undoubtedly their opinion stems from Roja's old history of Toledo.) It is known that the Jews were so numerous in Toledo that they created many small towns nearby, which at one time were totally Jewish. Such towns as Quintana de la Orden and Talavera de la Reina are known to have converted en masse in 1492.

The first evidence of the ancient Hebrews in Spain is to be found at Sadaba, Saragossa, where there exist the remains of a synagogue built approximately in the year 250 CE; the Roman influence in its design is fully apparent. The first evidence of Jews in Portugal appears in the form of an inscription of the sixth or seventh century found at Espiche, near Lagos, by the Belgian engineer Schwarz, which names Rabino Issac Hacohen, Rab Moshnuma, and Cohen ben Karbin.

Although Jewish settlements in Spain were visited by the Apostle Paul, the first written evidence of Jews in Spain is to be found in the legislation of the Council of Elvira (near Granada) which took place from 303 to 306 CE. This was probably the first national church council in Spain to legislate on Jews; in fact, it was probably the first anywhere so to legislate. The importance of the Elvira decrees is that they foreshadow the attitude of later church councils toward Jews. They also indicate that the break between Christianity and its parent Judaism had already become definitive.

1. *Before the Common Era* (BCE) and *Common Era* (CE) are the designations ordinarily used in histories of Jews and things Jewish. The eras correspond, respectively, to B.C. and A.D.

1

Moreover, in 415 CE and again in 423 CE Theodosius II interdicted the building of new synagogues or the repair and embellishment of existing ones. Justinian not only reinforced these restrictions, in 535 he commanded the wholesale destruction of synagogues in Africa.

Under the Visigoths, who took the peninsula from the Romans, life for the Jews was not pleasant. Recared (586-601), the first Visigothic king to become a Catholic, ruled that the children of any union between Hebrew and Christian must be baptized. The development of the Visigothic code from that time made it progressively harsher toward the Jews. Sisebut in 616 CE gave them the choice of baptism or emigration, with the result that many emigrated, especially to North Africa; the rest were given a time limit to become practicing Christians. They did so, but only to outward appearance. Within the sanctity of the family they remained Jews, thus becoming the first Marranos.[2] The Visigothic policy fluctuated from time to time, some rulers showing leniency, but in 652 Receswinth set a new time limit for conversion (apparently Sisebut had not had total success). Under Ervigio the Twelfth Council of Toledo put forth twenty-eight anti-Jewish laws which if carried out would have amounted to complete intolerance: the Jews must recant their faith, their property would be confiscated, and for any infringement of the law their hair would be cropped and they would automatically be punished by whipping. The last applied to Jews and to new converts. Finally Egica proposed in 694 that all Jews be reduced to slavery and distributed among the Christians, expressly prohibiting their liberation. In regard to synagogues, the buildings were tolerated, but only those already in existence could remain standing and not even repair was permitted. No new construction was allowed, which was a continuation of the policy of Theodosius. The Visigothic code influenced Catholic Spain all through the Middle Ages, and also influenced the Inquisition, which began at the time of the first Marranos.

Fortunately for the Jews this legislation was not always carried into effect, for the royal authority met with opposition in many parts of Spain. Further, the Visigoths had no capacity for commerce and needed the Jews because the peninsula until 1480 was sadly

2. *Marrano* possibly comes from *maran atha* ("our Lord has come") in the New Testament. Marranos were sometimes called Judaizing Christians or crypto-Jews.

underpopulated. This is not to say that all Jews were tradesmen and merchants; the majority of them were probably farmers, as they had been historically, and they probably existed in all strata of society except the nobility. In any event, it is not difficult to perceive why they actively helped the Moors conquer Spain.

To reward the Jews for being a fifth column, the caliphs of Córdoba treated them most kindly. Under the Moors, Jews became knights, physicians, scholars, and poets. There was even a Jewish prime minister when Córdoba was the largest city in the world. Jews established centers of learning (yeshiboth) in Toledo, Córdoba, Granada, Barcelona, and Lucena (which was then an all-Jewish city). They governed themselves in their juderías, with the rabbi as their chief. The years following 711 are known as the Golden Age of Judaism.

But in the twelfth century there arose the Almoravides, Moslem religious fanatics who instituted pogroms. About forty synagogues were burned. It was at this time that the great philosopher Maimonides was taken by his family to Egypt. Many other Jews fled the caliphate of Córdoba, going to the more tolerant Christian kingdom of Castile and the northern provinces. For the next century, at least, Toledo became the center of Judaism, producing such illustrious lights as Judah Halevy. It was at this time, in the 1100's, that the first king of Portugal issued decrees concerning Jews.

In 1265 under Alfonso X (the Wise) of Castile there was promulgated *las siete partidas,* the seven-part code, which concerned Jews. Of interest to this study is law number four on synagogues. It permitted the building of no new ones except by royal decree, unless it was a case of rebuilding to the same size as formerly existed. The law also prevented the painting of synagogues in all cases. This last portion was probably meant to prevent embellishment or grandeur, since it was common practice elsewhere to paint not only wood but also stone. The climate of Spain is such that paint is not needed as a preservative for wood.[3] At this time the Moors were not allowed to have mosques, so it can be inferred that the Jews were not on the bottom of the social scale. In fact, some Jews were quite wealthy and were requested to dress more plainly so as not to excite the envy of the balance of the population. At this time, too, laws were passed stating that only the nobil-

3. See examples described on pp. 40 and 65 regarding Tudela and Paredes de Nava.

ity could wear jewelry, which by implication restricted the Jews, who were not of the nobility. Under Alfonso X, the aljama of Toledo built the largest and most beautiful synagogue in all of Spain. But in 1311 the Council of Vienne decreed in Article II of its constitution: "synagogues that have been newly erected or enlarged shall be restored to their former state."

In 1391 Vicente Ferrer, the fanatical Christian monk, incited the populace to pogroms; thousands of Jews were killed or converted and hundreds of synagogues were burned. To rebuild Judaism, the rabbis asked every grouping of ten or more families to construct a new synagogue. Apparently most of the Jews were still farmers, and many lived in small communities in rural villages. Walled ghettos started about this time, but were never extensive on the Iberian peninsula. By 1415 much had been rebuilt when Pope Benedict XIII issued from Avignon a bull to close all synagogues recently repaired or rebuilt, permitting only one synagogue (the smallest) to remain open in any community. In 1465 this became the state policy in Castile and León under Henry IV. In 1480 Jews were again permitted to build, but only by royal decree. Once again on March 31, 1492, they were given the choice of conversion or exile, and this blow ended the Jewish community in Spain for 443 years.

Many of the Jews of Spain went to join their brethren in Portugal, only to meet harsh measures there in 1496. In 1508, under pressure from Spain, Portugal followed suit by exiling the Hebrews, but she recanted to some extent at the end of the 1600's. In the 1880's at Ponta Delgada on the island of São Miguel in the Azores there were three congregations with two rabbis (one of them existed without a rabbi, it seems) that had been formed by immigrants from North Africa. They were quite successful as traders, but their children intermarried, converted, or migrated, so that the Jewish community there no longer exists. Later in the nineteenth century the Jews of Lisbon received official permission to build a synagogue which is still standing today. In 1927 the Jews of Braganza prayed in the house of J. Albino Lopes Borges. In addition, there are at present congregations in Pôrto, Barcelona, and Madrid. There are, too, many Marranos to be found today in northern Portugal.

Certainly the ancient Hebrews have left a legacy in the land, the people, and the language. For example, the Portuguese and Spanish *sábado* comes from the Hebrew *sabbath*. In fact, the Span-

"There Remains a Look About the Eyes"

ish historian Enrique Ballesteros has stated, "The language of Moses had more influence on Castilian than did the idiom of Cicero."[4]

It is estimated that at least 500,000 Jews left Spain in 1492 and that perhaps an equal number converted, and since the total Spanish population at that time was not much over three or four million, most Spaniards are said to have Jewish blood. To this day one still finds in common usage the family names of Levi, Benjamín, Cortés, Miro, López, and Franco, all known to be formerly Jewish, all practicing Catholics now. The given names of Esther and Samuel are not uncommon. There is still today a saying in Spain, *De Hervas Judíos los mas*, which freely translates, "Everyone in Hervas is a Jew." Probably the formerly large Jewish population converted en masse. One old woman resident of the judería of Hervas informed the author (in 1966) that she had relatives who went to Holland a long time ago (a very large number of the émigrés of 1492 did go to Holland). Of course, all the residents of Hervas are today Catholics, but there remains "a look about the eyes."[5] The love of learning that prevailed among the ancients—every man among them could read and write—can be seen in the standard curriculum for a Spanish-Jewish male in the Middle Ages: literature, grammar, law, philosophy, medicine, religion, and mathematics through series functions, a formal education terminating at about age nineteen or twenty and indicating a high level of scholastic achievement at that time. Throughout Spain there remain Streets of the Jews, Streets of the Synagogue, Jewish Quarters, and Gates of the Jews —each a memory of a glorious heritage.

4. *Estudio histórico de Avila.* Quoting García Ayuso, Severo Catalina and others, he contends that Spanish grammar is closer to Hebrew than to Latin.
5. Morris and Hofer, *The Presence of Spain*, p. 15.

2. ORIGIN OF THE SYNAGOGUE

Within the foregoing historical framework we might well ask, what sort of religious buildings did the Jews erect? In this context, let us consider the origin of the synagogue as a building type, about which there are three theories.

The word *synagogue* is derived from the Greek *synagoge* ("assembly") or *synagein* ("to assemble, to gather"). This led Professor Salo Baron of Columbia University to deduce a socio-economic origin. He stated: "The geographical heterogeneity of the land of Israel, the economic self-sufficiency of the ancient towns, the weakness of central government agencies, strong autonomous municipal administration, local self-government by representative elders—all these fostered an early sense of self-reliance and self-rule among Jews. Early pre-exilic voluntary and forced dispersion brought about an adaptation of native forms to foreign conditions. The Deuteronomic revolution (621 BCE) brought about a centralization of sacrificial worship at the Temple of Jerusalem by abolishing local cult areas. After the return from the Babylonian Exile, the second religious revolution initiated by Ezra stimulated new forms of communal worship based on prayer, recitation of communal lore, liturgical song and sermon. These elements helped to transform the synagogue into an easily adaptable and portable institution which ultimately any ten Jewish men could establish anywhere in the world."[1]

S. Zeitlin, another Jewish scholar, carried this thought even further when he wrote "The returning exiles from Babylonia convened an assembly to arbitrate economic and social problems and called the participants Bnai Knesseth (sons of the assembly), the head of it Rosh Knesseth (head of the assembly), and the house in which they gathered Beth Knesseth (house of assembly), synagogue in Greek. These assemblies became permanently established and finally resulted in the institution of the synagogue."[2] His conclusion was that the origin of the synagogue was not for prayer, nor for study, but that it had a sociopolitical basis in community life.

Yet there are strong arguments for considering the synagogue

1. *The Jewish Community*, 6:89.
2. *Proceedings*, pp. 69-83.

7

most essentially as a house of prayer. On the bema (the reader's platform) we find the reader's table, which is symbolic of the table for the showbread (unleavened bread) that was in the forecourt of the Temple of Jerusalem. All the temples (there were at least six of them outside of Jerusalem) were built for sacrificial ceremony, and there are references in Roman records to offerings being brought to a synagogue. There is, too, a strong argument for prayer as a substitute for sacrifice. In such a vein the synagogue has been called a mikdash méat (small sanctuary, as in Córdoba), and it is often viewed as a substitute for the ancient temple. Its sanctity is not derived from its location, nor from its structure, nor from its furnishings. In the synagogue "God stands in the midst of the congregation," in the soul of man which has become the "Temple of the Lord."[3]

An equally strong argument can be made for labeling the synagogue as a house of study. The very word *Torah* (the five Books of Moses) means "to study," as the word *Talmud* (the Hebrew code of laws) means "to learn." Certainly Jews study and interpret law in their synagogues, a practice emulated by the early Christians but later dropped. The tie between synagogue and learning is so strong that in the time of Christ the synagogue served as a theological high school, or at least every synagogue was associated with a high school. The leader of the services no longer offered sacrifices, but was instead a teacher. "In place of the prophets came the wise."[4]

Probably all three theses are correct, and it is proper to consider the synagogue simultaneously as a beth tefillah (house of prayer), a beth midrash (house of study), and a beth knesseth (house of assembly). In corroboration, there is a synagogue stone, *circa* 60 BCE, found in Jerusalem, that has a Greek inscription which Landsberger has translated as "Theodotus, son of Vettenos, priest and archisynagogus, son of an archisynagogus, grandson of an archisynagogus, built the synagogue for the reading of the law and for the teaching of the commandments, furthermore the hospice and the chambers and the water installation, for the lodging of needy strangers."

3. Holisher, *The Synagogue and Its People.*
4. Abrahams, *Jewish Life in the Middle Ages,* p. 366.

3. DEVELOPMENT OF ARCHITECTURAL FORM

It is sensible to follow the famous architectural historian, Richard Krautheimer, in postulating a rational argument for the development of the architectural form of the synagogue, as he did in the introduction to his work, *Mittelalterliche Synagogen*.

One cannot consider the synagogue form without first studying its antecedent, the temple, and the transition from one to the other clearly shows the evolution of the Jewish culture. At first each head of a patriarchal unit could be his own priest, usually making his offering on an outdoor altar; then a priestly class evolved, officiating at rites in the temple; finally the sacrificial priests were set aside as a wholly new concept was gradually formed, that of an entire congregation directly involved with God. Thus, to replace the temple built for the stylized ritual prescribed in Leviticus came the synagogue in which the congregation's chief concern was God's word.

So, before the synagogue there was the temple. And Solomon's temple was in essence a religious architectural type in that every antique temple was thought of as a palace of God. The Egyptian temples, for example, were conceived as were palaces of emperors or sultans, containing many rooms, such as offices and living rooms of the king's servants (the priests), with storerooms, pantries, and all other essential spaces. The chamber of the deity was the focal point of the gigantic complex. The believers had access to the palace courtyard, where they assembled as would a group awaiting the arrival of the king. As the king's palace developed from a primitive home, so did the godly palace. The entire complex can be traced back to the original walled courtyard, the wide assembly room, and the innermost chambers.

The fundamental form of the Greek temple, however, was the megaran, the archaic home. Modifications of this simple hut consisted first of enlargement and then of the addition of a pillared entrance. The concept here was not of an omnipotent emperor or sultan, but rather of God as a small city king or baron. God lived within his smallish palace and was approached through his image. The believer stood in front of the dwelling place and in front of the dwelling place lay the altar on which the offering was placed. Only the consecrations were preserved in the temple. Later, as the

9

temple was enlarged, the god was moved back into his own cella, and the larger part of the inner room remained free and uncluttered for the use of the believers, no longer the sole domain of the priest.

The Jewish temple, which is described in 1 Kings, chapters 6, 7 (14-51), 8, was quite clearly conceived as the residence of the deity, and bears a resemblance to both the Greek and Egyptian forms. The focal point of Solomon's temple was the innermost chamber which was approached by the priests from the courtyard through a hall. While the priests placed an offering on the large altar in the inner chamber, the people remained in the courtyard with its two rows of columns. The temple was built as a rectangular prism 60 x 20 x 30 cubits, the last third being the holiest of holies which was only 20 cubits high instead of 30, and was entered through two doors. The holy ark, which contained the stone Mosaic tablets, was guarded herein by two winged cherubim.

The remainder of the inner temple was a less holy room which served as an anteroom for the deity. Here stood the gold-plated table for the showbread and the ten golden candlesticks, a small golden altar, and the other items described in 1 Kings 7:50. Surrounding this part of the edifice were the progressively smaller storage rooms on three levels with their winding stairs and slit windows. The entrance hall, as wide as the building and 10 cubits deep, came before the less holy room. In front of the hall stood the two columns, Joachim and Boaz.

The Israeli architect Jacob Jehuda spent several years building a model of the temple which was exhibited in the New York World's Fair of 1939. While amplifying the preceding description, it clearly showed the large features: the most holy separated behind the less holy chamber with its entry hall; in front of the house the courtyard with the altar; and the several annexes described in 2 Kings 23:7. The essential fact is that the God-servant placed himself in front of the master's house so that it should appear that God took up the offering from his throne in the inner cella while the people looked on.

It is questionable that only the high priest had the right of access to the holiest of holies in Solomon's temple. The culture of Solomon's time was so strongly patriarchal that the fundamental concept continued that every *pater familias* could assume the functions of a priest. Just before building the temple, "Solomon came to Jerusalem and stood before the ark of the covenant of the Lord, and

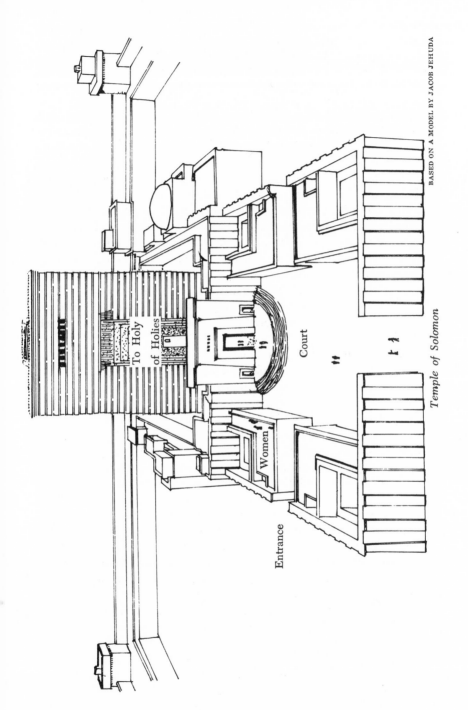

To Holy of Holies

Court

Women

Entrance

Temple of Solomon

BASED ON A MODEL BY JACOB JEHUDA

offered up burnt offerings" (1 Kings 3:15). Undoubtedly as family head of all his people he continued this practice. Only at the consecration did Solomon make the offering on the large altar in the forecourt (1 Kings 8:64), and as king he could certainly enter at least the less holy room. But to the people the less holy room surely remained closed, even though the strong division between the priestly class and laymen was not yet formulated.

The second temple, which was consecrated 516 years after the Babylonian exile, was apparently a fairly good copy of Solomon's temple. The liturgical rules were further evolved. The class distinctions between priest and laymen were delineated, and the hierarchy rules were prescribed. Ezra's reform in the middle of the fifth century codified this state. Thenceforth no priest except the high priest could approach the most holy, and the laymen could not enter the house of God. Those passages in Chronicles that stress the priestly privileges were written in Ezra's time. Only the priests, the court officials or king's civil servants so to speak, might approach the throne of the God-king.

It is reasonable to believe that when David allegedly gave Solomon the plans for the Temple (1 Chronicles 28:11) he based them on existing examples, or at least they grew out of that which was native to Judaism, that is, those sacred buildings which arose in previous Palestinian construction. Archeological evidence indicates that sacred buildings evolved slowly and patiently after about 1400 BCE, as 1 Kings, chapters 2 and 3, report. Originally the worship was out in the open, under the free sky, around a holy stone or a trunk standing on a pedestal. The offering was placed on an altar and the blood was poured into an offering trench in front of rows of uniform masses, perhaps as many as ten such chunks in the rows. Housing for the offerings would have blocked their access to heaven, and certainly was not necessary. However, a large number of buildings did contain high holy rooms. For example, in the old fort temple of Meggido, which Schumacher places in the second half of the third thousand years, the cult center was located in the center of a court that was surrounded by construction consisting of a room in the east and three smaller ones in the west. About one thousand years later a very similar holy place was built in Tell-es-Safy. The prototype changes only with the longevity of the locale of the religious cult-places, so long at least as the religion which created it does not experience essential change.

An interesting corroboration of this thesis may be found in the temple at Petra, which was built during the days of Imperial Rome. In Petra's temple the holy table plays an important role in providing a place for the meal offering. Although such a table is lacking in Palestinian temples, there must have been in them an opportunity for the meal offering to be presented. Consider the oldest part of the Old Testament, the Books of Judges and Samuel, wherein several passages are concerned therewith: in the prayer of the childless Hannah in Shiloh, and by Samuel when he takes Saul up to the high holy place at mealtime. Of course it is possible to eat in the open air, but undoubtedly in the case of Saul and Samuel a dining room is specified. Thus, the excavation of the holy chambers indicates that a building adjacent to the site of the worship was used for the meal offering. The other rooms would have been storerooms or living quarters for the priests.

In summary, before Solomon's temple and even up to Ezra's worship reform, the predominate form of worship site was a place of high holiness which was not encased in a God-house and in which buildings played a secondary role. Although often from the beginning the God's house stood in the middle of the complex, it is in this background that the familiar Solomonic temple stands *circa* 1000 BCE.

At the time this temple was built Judaism was not monotheistic. The Ten Commandments state "no other gods *before* me," and not just "no other gods." In the temple itself, near the revered box which contained Moses's stone tablets, Solomon placed a brazen snake and a sun horse, according to the priestly edition (*circa* 400) of the Book of Kings. Such images openly show godly honor. In his old age Solomon even built shrines to pagan gods to please some of his thousand wives and concubines, but it is unreasonable to believe that the snake and horse would be taken into the temple long after it was built. In spite of that, one new fact emerges: the worship image is in another sense God, it is as essentially personal as the stone or the tree trunk. So it demands even more its home, the residence in which it could be worshiped. With the worship, the image irrevocably involves the building of the temple. The same causal relationship exists in every religion.

Whether the Jews brought the temple form and the God-presentation with them from Egypt, or whether they adopted them from neighboring lands is moot. They did bring the ark with them; however, the ark is not an image but rather a God-symbol as the incarnation of Jehovah, and it is extremely doubtful that it ever got housing during the Bedouin period of Israel. Yet it is certain that temples in a real sense were existing in the time of the Judges, in the twelfth and eleventh centuries. In the Book of Judges, the seventeenth chapter unimpeachably speaks of this: a man named Mica in the tribe of Ephraim had a God-image in his own God-house with his own priest, and the situation is confirmed even though the other passages on the God-houses in Mizpah, Sichem, and Beth-El are not so clear. (Beth-El, by the way, literally means "house of God.")

Solomon's temple acted as a unifying effort toward monotheism by pushing the other temples into the background and acting as the large central holy place. Yet it was not native or indigenous. Besides Egyptian influence, concepts came from the Euphrates that formed the worship place—the house of God with cella and entry hall opposing the courtyard, and in the hall the altar, the brazen sea, and the transportable kettle. The architectural form and adornment are immaterial.

The temple form was unaltered for Judaism wherever it was constructed. After the beginning of the sixth century a garrison of Jewish soldiers in service to the Pharoah were stationed in upper Egyptian Elephantine, and they had a temple there similar to the one in Jerusalem. Another was built in the second century in Leontopolis in lower Egypt; a third stood in Borion in North Africa; and others were supposed to have been in Antioch and in the region of Damascus. In any event, there was not just one temple.

Even today in the religious worship places of the Falashis (the Abyssinian Jews) we see the first temple rather crudely handed down. The form is quite changed under the influence of surrounding peoples, but the important features remain.

Although it is possible to trace the development of the temple quite nicely, the origin of the synagogue is rather obscure. One cannot pinpoint the date of its origin. Probably certain passages in the Bible refer to synagogues, particularly those dating from the Babylonian exile, from the sixth century. For example, Ezekiel 11:1 speaks of a mikdash méat or small sanctuary, but since other interpretations can be placed on that phrase, it cannot be inferred that specific reference was made therein to a synagogue. Psalm 74 speaks of the destruction of "all the houses of God in the land," so it is certain that synagogues appeared in Palestine no later than the

time of the Maccabees, two centuries before Christ. A Greek dedication inscription of a synagogue was found in Schedia, Egypt,
dating from 250 BCE, and another in Alexandrionesus, in lower
Egypt, dates from the year 217 BCE. A good assumption would be
that synagogues gradually took form in the time after Ezra, after the
return from the Babylonian exile.

The development of the synagogue as an institution is of even
greater significance than its architectural form. The significance of
this creation, which grew alongside the temple, is that it indicates a
complete change in the Jewish concepts of religion. The final
product of the evolution was totally different from its origin. The
entire installation to God was changed in total depth. God was no
longer the emperor, the king, the baron, the master, to whom gifts
were proffered to gain favor. No longer was the ritual rigidly prescribed: the people standing in the distance, the Levites singing in
a chorus led by Asaph's descendants, and the priests performing in
step and cadence, all strictly in accord with written rules and regu-
lations. No longer was there the true ritual offering bound to the
particular place, Zion: the temples at Elephantine and in Leontopolis were only ersatz for the destroyed or desecrated temple in
Jerusalem, at least in the eyes of the true-believing priests there.
Now it was possible for the ordinary Israelites to come together at
any place that Jews resided. From then on the words of Jesus were
understood (as the Dead Sea Scrolls indicate, he stood throughout
within the mainstream of Jewish thought): "Wherever two or three
come together in my name, there I am with them." Each synagogue
was an independent establishment of the people, a popular creation
to satisfy the needs of the masses, owing allegiance to no one person
or institution. The synagogue had no privileges to offer to any social
group, to state officials, or to members of a priesthood. It possessed
the features of a democratically organized unit grounded in the
common people. Every person was considered equal before God in
the synagogue.

It is possible that prayer substituted for sacrifice, but at least of
equal importance with prayer is the study and interpretation of
scripture. The word walks in place of the act. With the conception
of a house of learning in contrast to a house of God devoted to
offerings, an entirely new problem was posed for architectural solu-
tion. Holisher states that the synagogues constituted the first formal
school buildings the world had ever seen, hence there were no ar-

chitectural antecedents. Obviously, it was impossible to put the new God-servant in a building which, like the temple, was just patterned on the offering servant as the summit of the worship business. God was no longer thought of as a person. One no longer approached him in a ceremonial manner, for this would require him to be localized in an all-holiest specific location. Instead his presence becomes purely spiritual, he is over all and nowhere. The tendency toward this thought was perhaps first put forth by an inspired King Solomon (1 Kings 8:27), but now the believers gather together to hear God's word from those who are learned in scripture. Then the lecturer must be visible to all, so it is necessary to create a building which contains a centrally located, elevated platform around which the believers can gather. This raised platform, called a bema, becomes the spiritual and local center.

With this background let us now consider the development of the synagogue in Iberia. It would not be reasonable to state that the existence of the "room around the bema" was considered essential and after this consideration was designed and executed. That particular room form grew out of the conditions which formulated it, without deliberate consideration and knowledgeable design. By trial and error the appropriate shape was found and became definitive until such time as the religious disposition, evidenced by a change in rite and ritual, demanded a new form. The shape was based on that which was known as a religious building, i.e., the temple. Generally a simple rectangular basilica, it often had rows of columns, as in the great synagogue of Alexandria, or later as in Segovia and in Santa María la Blanca in Toledo. The only prerequisites were a space for the bema and another for the ark or chest containing the Scrolls of the Torah.

At first every ark was portable within the synagogue (the Talmud states: "Do not leave the synagogue until the Scrolls of the Law have been removed" [Sota 39b]), but it was probably placed in view of the worshiper in accordance with Solomon's prayer (1 Kings 8:30) on which is based the Talmudic dictum: "When praying in exile, face Israel; when in Israel, face Jerusalem; when in Jerusalem, face the temple; and when in the temple, face the east." For example, the synagogue at El-Hammeh, Israel, has its rounded apse at the south. Perhaps for lack of a better storage space, the ark became a permanent fixture within the synagogue and was always placed on the east wall rather than precisely toward Jerusalem. This particular orientation may simply have been devised to achieve a uniformity so that the traveler would feel at home wherever he went, or perhaps, with the destruction of the second temple in 71 CE and the grave doubts concerning its rebuilding, every synagogue was indeed a mikdash méat, a small sanctuary, a temporary miniature of the temple. Blocking the east wall could not have been accomplished originally, since the first synagogues had their entrances and some windows on that exposure to agree with Daniel 6:11: "And when Daniel knew that the writing was signed, he went into his house—now his windows were open in his upper chamber toward Jerusalem—and he kneeled upon his knees three times a day and prayed and gave thanks before his God as he did aforetime." The importance of the permanent ark demanded at least a niche in the wall, as at Córdoba, if not an apse, rounded as at Elche or angular as at Avila. In any event, the Scrolls of the Law were always elevated above the assembly, and a few steps occur at the foot of the ark.

The relationship of the bema to the ark has never been fixed. From the Babylonian and Jerusalem Talmuds, Krauss infers that the bema was in the center of a large colonnaded hall in Alexandria. Projecting out from that wooden bema was a keren (horn), a ledge on which the khazzan (reader) stood. It is interesting to note that whenever the Scrolls of the Law were raised aloft during services, or whenever a benediction was recited, the reader waved a sudarion (kerchief) as a signal to the worshipers, and the congregation responded with "Amen." The centrally located bema was undoubtedly also to be found in Portugal, as evidenced by the plan of the synagogue of Tomar: the square room contains four central columns defining an inner square. From Portugal the Jews migrated to Denmark, thence to Poland, and in Poland the almost universal practice was to place a square bema in a central location, with a column at each of its four corners, a theme which was repeated in the later "Portuguese synagogue" in Amsterdam. Hence, it can be inferred that the bema was contained within the columns at Tomar. A similar disposition is found today in the Lisbon synagogue. In Spain, on the other hand, it is more reasonable to believe that the bema was located along the opposite wall from the ark whenever practicable. In 1492 many Jews migrated from Spain to Italy, and in the so-called Spanish synagogues in Italy at Padua, Pesaro, Ferrara, and Venice, all of which were built early in the 1500's, we find the ark on one side and the bema on the other, projecting into the assembly room. Furthermore, in Córdoba we find on the wall across from the niche of the ark rich ornamentation enclosing a blank space. That space was probably filled with a chair for the khazzan, or the back of a pulpit. Hence, the bema was on one side, the ark on the other.

The walled forecourt reminiscent of the Jerusalem temple was incorporated into the synagogue complex whenever space permitted. At times it was quite small, as at Córdoba, and at times of goodly size, as at Medinacelli, or it might have been an interior space as at the Hermendad in Toledo. In addition to being a quasi-public square where the congregants gathered to gossip before and after religious services, it could have served as the locale of a legal forum to settle disputes among Jews without resorting to civil courts of law whose decisions could prove expensive to both parties. It possibly served also as the site of a succah (booth), a temporary structure erected for the harvest festival, and it was used for other festive occasions. In any event, on one side it was flanked by the all-important midrash (schoolhouse) for both young and old, and on the other side was a social hall or an institution housing the way-farer and the stranger, unless these spaces had been incorporated into the synagogue building.

4. THE INTERIOR

Whether by law, by edict, or by design, the synagogue exterior on the Iberian Peninsula was generally quite plain and simple. Perhaps there existed a desire for anonymity, the congregation hoping that if the building were inconspicuous, it would not be damaged during times of trouble; or perhaps the façades were simply designed in the fashion of the day. There existed of course the previously cited code that prohibited the painting of synagogues, but the prohibition could have been circumvented with carving, tile work, and pattern embellishment on the brickwork. That this was not done indicates perhaps a certain humility. Yet, architecturally, the synagogue was the most imposing structure in the judería, built generally in Moorish design, sometimes also Gothic. In fact, according to local legend some of the synagogues had been originally mosques which the Christian conquerors presented to their Jewish subjects as a sign of favor or gratitude, such as Cristo de la Luz in Toledo. Although the synagogue was higher than the surrounding residences, it was by law and Catholic influence kept lower than its neighboring church. In 1221 Pope Honorius III ordered the Archbishop of Burgos to destroy the new synagogues which had been erected in his province contrary to canonical decrees.

The richness of the interiors varied with the wealth of the donors or congregants. In some the plaster was magnificently carved, as at Córdoba and El Tránsito at Toledo, in others it was left plain and smooth, as at Cáceres and Tomar. Since Jews were to be found throughout the spectrum of Spanish and Portuguese life, some were poor, a few were rich, and most got along as well as did their neighbors. Hence of the hundreds, perhaps thousands of synagogues which existed (Seville alone, with a Jewish population of six to seven thousand families, had twenty-three synagogues before they were destroyed in 1391), a few could be expected to be quite expensively finished, while most were probably rather simple. The ark was always richly adorned, at least with some silver where the ark was built of wood, if not adorned by carving in plaster; universally it had on it an inscription. The bema too was probably an object of decoration.

19

The limited size of the interior posed a seating problem. When a new synagogue was built, the elders of the community assigned seating space in accordance with social standing, either to families or, more often, to individuals with full proprietary title and the privilege of transfer by gift, sale, or bequest. The individuals then furnished their own seats, in reflection of their own taste and wealth, so that the same room would contain carved stone benches, wooden seats, and loose pillows on the floor. The family or individual name would be inscribed on the seat, a practice still followed in the Sephardic synagogues of London, Lisbon, and Venice. The nineteenth-century historian E. H. Lindo wrote: "At times, the traffic in synagogue seats was so active that it was possible to create a quasimonopoly and an artificial price inflation which the Aljama [Jewish community] had to counteract. Newcomers or those who were not fortunate enough to share in the original partition of the synagogue were barred from setting up temporary chairs or spreading a carpet matting in the center of the auditorium. They had, however, the privilege of renting from the more fortunate members the seats which were not in use; and if necessary, the communal authorities intervened forcibly in their behalf with stubborn seat-holders. The synagogue officials ruled with iron control. Protests were unavailing, and heavy fines were imposed on those who insisted on occupying seats which were assigned to others. It is curious and significant to find the monarch himself, King Pedro IV, intervening in behalf of his jeweler, Guedaliah Avenarama of Saragossa, to secure for him the coveted privilege of erecting two seats in the synagogue of Calatayud."[1] (Two seats were all that Avenarama needed, since children sat at the feet of their elders or wandered freely in unoccupied spaces.) It is obvious, therefore, why several synagogues were always built in the typical Jewish quarter.

Synagogues may have been built by the community as a whole, but more often they were probably sponsored by a guild, a special society, or an individual. There are apparently no records of any synagogue tax. Lovely houses of worship which are still standing were erected by individuals in Toledo and in Córdoba. In addition, records indicate that one in Toledo was paid for by Joseph ibn Shoshan, another in Seville by Joseph of Ecija; one in Barcelona was erected by Samuel Benveniste, and there was an Abenveniste

1. *The Jews of Spain and Portugal*, p. 149.

synagogue in Saragossa; while in Calatayud there was the Ibn Yahya edifice, besides two other chapels of prayer and study that bore the names of their founders. There were also countless individual rooms in private homes used exclusively for worship and study, similar to that of Oña, although in other locales they arose because of the limited seating available in the more formal structures and the restrictions on erecting buildings that were to be used solely as synagogues.

After the twelfth century women were always seated in a separate section in accordance with Jewish laws on cleanliness. At certain times of the month women are not permitted to share a bed with their husbands and would also at these times render their husband's prayers unclean; however, since for at least certain holy days attendance in a synagogue is well-nigh compulsory, it was necessary to reserve a separated area for them. Usually they were relegated to a balcony, as at Tudela, Paredes de Nava, and Córdoba; in other instances a portion of the hall was reserved for them. The second Jerusalem temple certainly had a women's gallery, for the *Mishnah* (commentary), Middot 2.5, speaks of a women's forecourt surrounded by a gallery, so that the women looked on from above and the men from below.

Whenever possible, lighting was accomplished by daylight streaming in through clear glass, for a synagogue lit up by sunlight was considered conducive to the mood of prayer. The preservation of privacy could then be accomplished by means of high windows, as in the synagogues in Toledo and that in Avila. Artificial lighting was accomplished by hanging oil lamps or candles probably similar to that found in the circumcision room in Lisbon today. The shape of the oil lamps can be seen in ancient documents, such as the fourteenth-century Spanish *Haggadah* (book of the Passover ritual) now in the National Museum, Sarajevo, Yugoslavia; the *Haggadah* in the British Museum, Or. 2884; and the Catalan painting "Jesus Among the Doctors," Friedsam Collection, Metropolitan Museum of Art, New York City, which shows the temple as a contemporary synagogue. In all cases the lamps hanging from a chain are identical in shape. Star-shaped lamps of bronze or brass were also used in synagogue interiors.

Color may have been used on the walls—traces of it are found on the walls of El Tránsito, Toledo—but even though the ancient synagogue of Dura Europos, Syria, had all walls covered with murals of Biblical scenes, undoubtedly nothing but geometric designs or lettering was used in Iberian Jewish buildings in strictest accord with the interpretation of the commandment interdicting graven images. Archeologist E. R. Goodenough feels that this iconoclasm did not take hold until about the seventh century CE.

Gate of the Jews

5. THE MEMORY REMAINS

Here and there in Spain, at least, there are to be found a Calle Judería as in Córdoba, or a Calle Judería Vieja as in Segovia; at times a Plaza de la Sinagoga as at Onda, or simply a Calle de la Sinagoga as in La Coruña and in Hervas. Certain towns such as Toro and Sagunto contain well-defined sections which are known to the present inhabitants to have been at one time the Jewish quarter and are still called the judería, but which contain no practicing Jews today. At times these quarters are entered through a Gate of the Jews and at times, as in Avila, they are simply a section of the town. The citizens know that at one time Spain was inhabited by a group called Jews, just as at one time there were Visigoths, Romans, and Moors on the land; there is no further significance for them.

There remain sayings, as the one about Hervas already quoted, and that which reads "Tomadlas de Villadiego," which means literally "take off to Villadiego," that is, to flee or escape there. It is believed that at one time Villadiego was a sanctuary for Jews. The local inhabitants could define no section of the town as a judería, although the Church of Madre Augustine was probably built on the site of a synagogue. Romanticists could form interesting speculations as to the origin of the saying.

More definitive and perhaps typical of ancient times is the still existing judería of Hervas. It is located downhill from the main town in the very old Roman section and is reached by passing through a gate in the city wall. Nearest the gate, in the highest portion of the judería, are the largest houses, handsome half-timbered structures which were probably owned by the wealthy. Farther down are the narrow cobblestoned streets with the plastered houses side by side, some streets devoid of sunlight, where donkeys still traverse and the women still go to the well for water. The streets are a filthy mess. Sheep, dogs, and donkeys pass through them daily, and the houses are squeezed together. In Toro to this day the streets in the judería are an open sewer wherein flows a slow black sludge of a stream.

It is possible that the judería was originally within the walls of Hervas. In 1480 the Jews (and the Moors too, for that matter)

23

Hervas, View of Jewish Section

were moved outside the walls of Avila, and a similar action might have taken place in Hervas around that time.

It was in such an atmosphere that most of the medieval Hebrews lived when in the cities. But when he entered his synagogue and put on his prayer shawl, a Jew became the equal of his fellows, a man among men. In such a context let us now consider those synagogues which remain, at least in part, to this day.

6. RUINS

We have written that the Jews first came to the Iberian Peninsula at a very early time, possibly as early as the eleventh century BCE. In 1492 the Jews of Spain were forcibly exiled or as forcibly converted, and the Jewish population of Portugal was ended the same way in 1508. It is not at all surprising, therefore, that ruins are all that remain of many of their synagogues. As a prelude to the description of those synagogues still standing, we shall take notice of two such ruins.

SADABA

The oldest remnant of any synagogue on the Iberian Peninsula may well be that found in Sadaba, Spain. Sadaba is a small town not far from France, situated about midway between the Mediterranean Sea and the Atlantic Ocean. Although the local inhabitants and the government state that the remains are those of a synagogue, Dr. Antonio García Bellido feels otherwise.[1] It is difficult to understand why Jews should settle in this place particularly, unless they came with the Romans as their slaves or perhaps as traders. Enrique Ballesteros in *Estudio Histórico de Avila* states that in the time of Vespasian large numbers of Jews took refuge in Spain, and that from the time of Caesar Augustus there were colonies of Jews in Spain. At any rate, by 200 CE the community of Sadaba apparently was of substantial size, and at least some Jews in it had attained a measure of wealth, judging by the synagogue ruins.

The remaining wall is completely of stone, a type of construction which does not seem to have been used by the Hebrews in any succeeding house of worship until the Great Synagogue of Avila was built more than 1,200 years later, possibly because of the excessive cost of such a building. The style of architecture indicates that it was built about two centuries after the birth of Christ. In Sadaba one notes the important theme of five which will be seen again and again in other locations. The reference is to the Torah, the five books of Moses in the Old Testament. The three gabled sections have no recognizable significance other than design

1. *Sefarad*, 22:436.

ornamentation. The picture shows the interior face of the eastern wall, which should have contained an ark. Close inspection of the central niche shows indentations similar and adjacent to a central hole, as though they might have held some wooden brackets to

Sadaba, Ruins

support an ark. The holes in each of the other four niches are difficult to explain. The somewhat worn Latin inscription indicates that two women had this edifice built with their own funds, which is unusual, since men generally donated money for this purpose. Perhaps the synagogue was constructed in fulfillment of a vow.

ELCHE

Let us now consider the ruins excavated at Elche (Ilici) in the province of Alicante, near the southeastern coast of Spain. The synagogue was built in an area which is at present a short distance outside the town, in what is now a lemon grove. This is not too surprising when one considers that the entire judería of Pôrto, Portugal, was located in an area which is now an olive grove, and a former synagogue in Cáceres, Spain, is well removed from the present city. The town of Elche was established by the Phoenicians (as evidenced by pottery excavated there) who brought Hebrews along with them.

The synagogue was not a very large building, just a simple rectangular prayer hall about 34 by 23 1/2 feet, with a rounded apse about 9 1/2 feet wide at the east end and an entrance on the west. The major axis was along the east-west line, and the rectangle was enlarged along this axis to include the apse at a later date, according to several archeologists. These men feel that the original synagogue had rooms added to it when it was converted into a church. By the evidence found elsewhere in Spain, this does not seem to be a reasonable conclusion. It would have been more logical for the Church to add an apse or, since there already was one, to remove it, extend the building, and then build a new apse, thus ridding the hallowed ground of the "abomination" which had stood there. Such was the type of action taken in Cáceres and in Paredes in later years. A better conclusion would be that the added rooms were used for study, for legal procedures, or for housing Jewish travelers who came to visit this synagogue.

The mosaic floor contained Greek inscriptions. The one along the north side runs eastward toward the apse and reads *archouts and presbyters*, which indicates that this area was reserved for the elders of the congregation. The central inscription, which runs across the hall at a distance of approximately ten feet from the apse, reads *proseuche* ("prayer house"), followed by a word in which only the letters *lao* are discernible. Rachel Wischnitzer argues that herein was found the name of the synagogue, *lao* having originally been *laos* ("people"), and one should read "Prayer House of the People of. . . ." The final inscription was on the south side, running westward, and reads *euplois* ("voyage, or fair voyage"); the letters which follow are obliterated. The entire statement may have alluded to a return to the Holy Land, similar to the plaque in Córdoba, or it may have signified the fulfillment of a vow concerning the safe return of certain Phoenician vessels. The geometric pattern of the balance of the floor seems to indicate that the bema was located in a central area adjacent to the central inscription, rather than on the northern wall as Mrs. Wischnitzer contends. If it had been on the north, then, when the Scrolls of the Law were opened, placed on the table, and read, the reader would be facing south, which is untenable for Elche, but quite correct in the Galilee region of Israel. The bema could not have been far from the ark, and the khazzan (reader) had the elders to his left when he read the Law while facing east.

Hervas, Street in Jewry

7. SMALL TOWNS

During the Middle Ages a large city such as Rome had only some 20,000 people. The entire Iberian Peninsula was underpopulated, which leads one to believe that the Jews were tolerated there until they were no longer deemed necessary in terms of the total number of inhabitants, and after that they were exiled. Although there were certain principal centers of Judaism—throughout Andalusia, and at Palencia, Plasencia, and Toledo—the Jews settled in every part of Spain. There is, for example, in a Castilian edict of 1234, ". . . it is ordained that all Jews in town or country. . . ." Cantera indicates records of over one hundred different synagogues, with no more than three in most towns. But there must surely have been many more than a hundred. We have already noted that Seville had twenty-three before 1391, Calatayud had seven and several private places of worship, and the eight in Valladolid were burned with that city during the war of 1367.

ONA

The smaller towns, rural villages really, had only one synagogue, and that one was likely to be a modest structure. In Oña the entire judería consisted of just one street which ran from the plaza downhill to the main road. The synagogue was located at the top of the street on the left side as one approaches the plaza. It is today a private residence and might possibly have been just that when it was used as a house of worship. The entrance is quite plain, just flat rubble stonework around a rectangular opening. The overhanging second floor is typical of homes of that era, as can be seen in Hervas and many other communities. Inside there is a gothic arch around a door which led to the prayer chamber. Because of subsequent remodeling on an extensive scale, it is difficult to determine the original plan of the synagogue.

LUCENA

A similar difficulty arises in Lucena. Here the synagogue was more impressive, for Lucena was a somewhat larger town, and even

Oña, Synagogue

Oña, Interior Doorway

Lucena, Courtyard of Synagogue

Lucena, Interior of Synagogue

boasted of a yeshiva for the training of rabbis. In the tenth century Lucena was a walled Jewish city. Of the many synagogues it undoubtedly had, only one remains, remodeled, considerably altered, and at present used for a tile factory. Even the street façade was altered, the style indicating work of the eighteenth century. The interior courtyard shows Moorish arches and some interior construction is Mozarabic, with its plaster arches between rough-hewn wooden joists. The thick brick walls have been stuccoed and white-washed many times in the intervening centuries. The original plan is indiscernible. Although the building is now 63 feet wide, it was originally 25 feet wider. There remains one room 45 feet by 12 feet, having a row of brick columns along one side, each column being 27 inches by 36 inches, with 8-foot arches on 8-foot spring lines between them supporting the beamed ceiling. There are several other rooms.

Map of Tomar

TOMAR

Another town whose judería consisted solely of one street is Tomar in Portugal. As the map shows, the Jews lived five blocks north of the grand square, and their synagogue was located on the south side of the street at its midlength. The plan of the building is somewhat of a puzzle. Since the courtyard had to be in either the northeastern or northwestern corner, it is difficult to understand why the former was chosen, necessitating an entrance on the eastern wall. The only explanation can be that such an arrangement is in accord with the previously cited lines from the Old Testament concerning Daniel's mode of prayer. As J. M. Santos Simões indicates in his excellent study, the room to the south of the courtyard was used to separate the women from the main hall, but may have been a later addition.

The sanctuary itself is rather small, measuring only 31 by 27 feet, with four slender stone columns supporting the groin vaults. With a window at the middle of both the north and south walls, perhaps the ark was movable and the bema was probably located in the center of the hall, surrounded by the columns. The style is that of the late fifteenth century in Portugal, being a blend of late French Gothic and Italian Renaissance. The capitals with their pleasant geometric ornamentation and the simply carved bases of the columns in the interior are obviously Gothic, but the wall brackets supporting the vaults are composed of cone-like flutings building up to egg-and-dart ornament between Ionic volutes. As Simões pointed out, this interior bears a strong resemblance to the crypt of the fifteenth-century Collegiate Church at Ourém.

The present exterior is a remodeling of a later date, the present door having originally been a window and the two flanking windows having been cut out of the original solid wall. The prayer hall is below the street level, recalling the Biblical quotation "From the depths do I call unto Thee," but it may be simply because of building settlement over the years. In 1921 the building was declared a national monument and was restored by the Portuguese government. In 1933 it was turned over to the Museo Luso-Hebraico, a museum dedicated to the memory of Abraham Zacuto (1450-1515), the exile from Spain who was court astronomer for King John II of Portugal. Today it houses many interesting stones unearthed from ancient graves and synagogues in Portugal.

Tomar, Synagogue Exterior

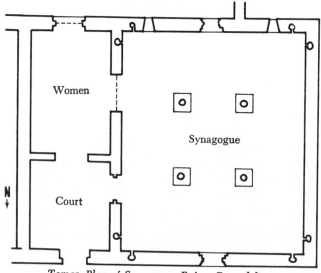

Tomar, Plan of Synagogue Before Remodeling

Tomar, Interior

MEDINACELLI

The synagogue of the hamlet is represented by that of Medina-celli, Spain, located a short distance from a main highway. The tiny mountaintop town is approached by a narrow road which at times seems to go straight up. At an edge of the high plateau is the Convent of Jerónimos, which is believed to have been a former synagogue, perhaps because of its proximity to the Calle de la Sinagoga. The building is locked and unused; the key is in possession of the bishop, who lives many miles away. It is a simple, low, brick structure, approached through a masonry fenced courtyard. It has no exterior ornamentation of any sort. The arched doorway, the small high windows of clear glass, the low profile, and the plan as evidenced by the external form, all give weight to the hypothesis as to its origin.

CACERES

The typical country synagogue, analogous to a country church, is the present church Espíritu Santo, on the outskirts of Cáceres. The original rectangular building was constructed in the 1200's, and the apse was added about three hundred years later. A further addition was built in 1962. Perhaps the quite pleasant porch on the south side of the structure was built in lieu of a courtyard, since the barren, rocky yard in front of it, which is now used by chickens to scrabble for food, contains no definite walls or fences.

While most of the structure is stucco on brick, both inside and out, the interior 6-foot-high columns are of stone supporting pointed brick arches. The problem of supporting arches with different spring lines was solved with unique multiple capitals. The tile roof is set on a wooden ceiling. The brick floor extends out as the porch floor. The total effect, within and without, is naïve and charming. The exterior plaster was tooled to look like stone on the pointed arches supporting the porch roof. Around the quite plain rectangular doorway stone trim was used.

The low height of the interior precluded a balcony. Perhaps the women sat in a separate section at the west end of the rectangular hall, which is about 40 feet by 58 feet. The ark was undoubtedly in a niche in the east wall before that wall was cut through for the added apse when the building was taken over in 1492. The bema

Medinacelli, Synagogue

Cáceres, Synagogue

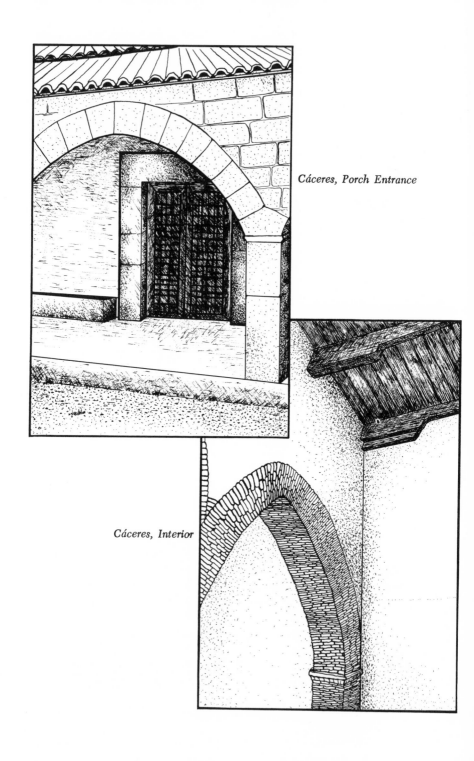

Cáceres, Porch Entrance

Cáceres, Interior

must have been in the central square defined by the columns. There were auxiliary buildings to the southeast and to the southwest which originally housed the school and the students. In any event, while the Jews on the outskirts of Cáceres were not at all wealthy, they had good taste.

Within the city itself, the judería exists and the residents thereof intermarried until after 1945. Whether or not they were Marranos cannot be determined. The Chapel of San Antonio is built on the site of a previous synagogue.

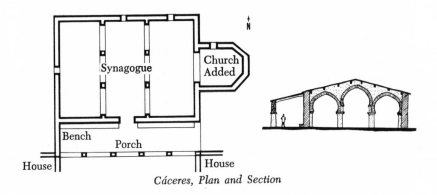

Cáceres, Plan and Section

Tudela

Because of the stone trim around its entrance and around its windows, the synagogue at Tudela is difficult to classify as that of a small town, yet it is certainly unpretentious, both in size and in height. The city itself was the birthplace of that intrepid traveler Benjamín who set out eight hundred years ago to find the lost ten tribes. He traveled as far east as Persia, going from one Jewish community to the next. He returned by way of North Africa and recorded his adventures in a marvelous travel book. In 1960 the citizens of Tudela erected a large terra-cotta plaque in his honor, twelve feet above street level, on a prominent square. Not far from the plaque is the Cathedral of Tudela, whose chapel on the north side of the cloister was formerly the synagogue. It is not unreasonable to believe that the northern portion of the cloister was at one time the southern porch of the synagogue, similar to that of Cáceres.

The rough stone "mosaic" floor has six-pointed stars in its corners, and an inexplicable stone remains below the central window of the façade. Was this stone part of a former bench, such as we find at Cáceres? The Jews of Tudela were of the same economic status as their brethren in Cáceres, for "the synagogue of Tudela being in need of repair, the King advanced them 120 livres, for which sum the Jewry was indebted to him."[1]

The façade of the chapel contains five windows, probably symbolic of the five books of the Torah, with a doubled pair set a short distance on either side of a central opening. The mullion of each of the paired windows is a short, round, stone column with a quasi-Ionic base and a capital carved in an interesting leaf form. The heads of the easterly pair are Arabic horseshoe arches, while those of the westerly pair are simple semicircles; in both cases they are, as a pair, representative of the tablets of the Ten Commandments. The larger central window also has a semicircular head ánd represents the oneness of God ("Hear, O Israel, the Lord our God, the Lord is one"). The westerly pair adjoin a Gothic doorway with a few carved moldings. The brick walls were stuccoed inside and out in the fashion of the time, but stone was used for trim around the windows and the door. Apparently the social climate of Tudela was hospitable to Judaism, for the windows are set unusually close to the ground, relative to the usual synagogue of that era. A tile roof carries on a wooden ceiling, which is supported by brick arches, and a brick floor completes the construction.

The entrance door opens into a small vestibule, another unusual feature. Opposite the vestibule is a stairway leading to the women's balcony (the women also had originally a private entrance on the north side of the building). The balcony must have been a splendid thing when it was first built, with panels of carved wooden grillwork set between decorated posts. Its wooden floor was carried by wooden joists supported by a decorated wooden beam and infillings. The original geometric patterns are still visible. Of course, no pictures would have been painted, but one might have expected to find some sort of quotation or dedication. Perhaps this was originally painted on the walls and has since been obscured with many coats of whitewash. The carved letters on the exterior stonework are a later addition, but the interior walls have carved into them a simple overall geometric pattern.

1. Lindo, *The Jews of Spain and Portugal*, p. 153.

Tudela, Synagogue Exterior

FOTO MAS

Tudela, Window Detail

FOTO MAS

Tudela, Interior   FOTO MAS

One last unusual feature should be noted. There is a small storage closet, about three feet high, with a wooden door under the interior staircase. Was this at one time a genizah, a storage for any book or document containing a reference to God, such as the one found by the Cambridge scholar Solomon Schechter in the ancient synagogue in Cairo in the late 1800's?

8. CITIES

Many of those Spanish cities which had a multiplicity of synagogues have swallowed up their past in their present, and no trace remains of those former buildings. In Seville, for example, it is known that the churches of San Bartolomé del Compás, Santa María de la Blanca, and Santa Cruz were all built on the sites of former Jewish houses of worship, but the houses were razed to their foundations before the present edifices were constructed. At Santa María de la Blanca the doorway was probably retained, but the interior has been rebuilt, if not extensively remodeled. The columns on either side of the door are attached round stone shafts without bases. Their capitals are carved in leaf form, topped by cones and central volutes, but the leaves do not have the veining exhibited at Tudela. The round-headed door leads directly to the interior.

In most of the centers of Judaism one of the synagogues was the sinagoga mayor, used solely as a beth knesseth, the others fulfilling the function of a beth midrash. At least three examples remain of such a great synagogue whose function was only that of a house of assembly, those three being in Segovia, Toledo, and Avila.

SEGOVIA

In Segovia the Church of Corpus Christi is located on the Calle Judería Vieja near the Cathedral. Corpus Christi was formerly a great synagogue. Erected prior to 1389, it was converted into the Iglesia Nueva in 1419. It got its present name in 1450.

Corpus Christi is entered through a Gothic doorway set in a beautifully patterned wall only 20 feet wide, which leads into a courtyard. The entrance to the synagogue itself is through a Moorish doorway above which is a paired window, similar to the easterly set in Tudela, except that the column mullion is much slimmer. Again we see the symbolism of the Ten Commandments. Inside is found a wooden floor and a Mudejar ceiling, with wood tie beams about 50 inches on center and wood joists with collar beams on 25-inch centers. The side aisles are separated from the nave by a set of five horseshoe arches resting on octagonal columns 30 inches in diameter, whose capitals are carved in a pine-cone motif. The east wall has a niche for the ark, and over the niche are five single windows,

Seville, Detail of Column

Seville, Synagogue Doorway

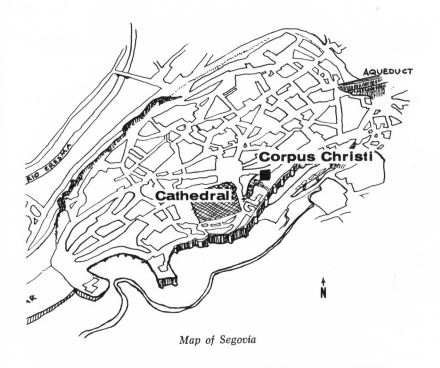

Map of Segovia

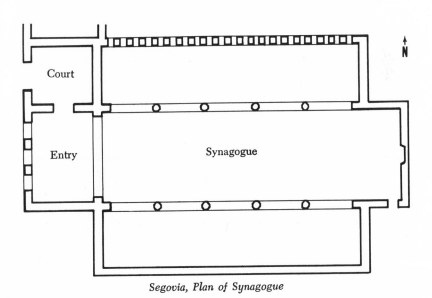

Segovia, Plan of Synagogue

each similar in shape to those at the entrance. The three different sets of five each allude to the five books of Moses, the Torah. The main hall measures 61 feet by 75 feet. Interestingly, the third-century synagogue at Capernaum, Palestine, is about the same size and also has two side aisles. The church was destroyed by fire in the late 1800's and rebuilt in 1899. At present it is attached to a convent.

TOLEDO—LA BLANCA

In Toledo the great synagogue is strikingly similar to Corpus Christi, except that, as can be seen from the map, La Blanca is quite removed from the Cathedral. Although cathedrals were usually built adjacent to the judería, it should be remembered that at least half the population of Toledo was Jewish and would not be contained in one small quarter. The square adjacent to La Blanca was only recently named the Plaza Judería. Furthermore, in the twelfth century Yehuda al-Harizi states in his *Takhemoni* his admiration for the number of synagogues in Toledo.

The history of Toledo's sinagoga mayor is well documented. Originally built about 1260 CE (a previous great synagogue was destroyed by fire in 1250), it was consecrated as a church in 1411, twenty years after the fanatical uprisings associated with Vicente Ferrer. In the second half of the sixteenth century the building was converted into the Convent of Santa María la Blanca. Three chapels were erected at the eastern end of the building in 1550. From 1791 to 1798 the building was used as an armory. In 1851 it was declared a national monument, and it was restored in 1856 under the direction of the architect Francisco Enríquez Ferrer. The building is alluded to in Jacob ibn Albeneh's Hebrew "Elegy on the Martyrs of Toledo, 1381."

Santa María la Blanca also differs from the Iglesia Corpus Christi in that it has doubled side aisles instead of single ones. These four aisles show a similarity to the ancient great synagogue of Alexandria. However, both in Segovia and in Toledo we find octagonal columns without bases, capitals carved as pine cones, horseshoe arches, and a Mudejar ceiling, and both synagogues are built of stuccoed brick. The carving in the stucco above the interior arches is quite elaborate in Toledo. Czekelius believes that the upper arcades were not always blank, but originally held windows which were sealed at a later date.

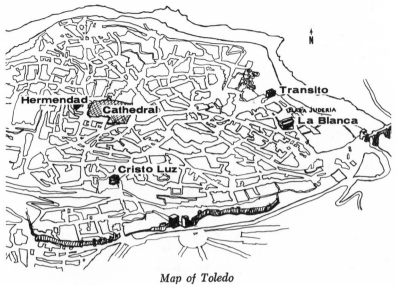

Map of Toledo

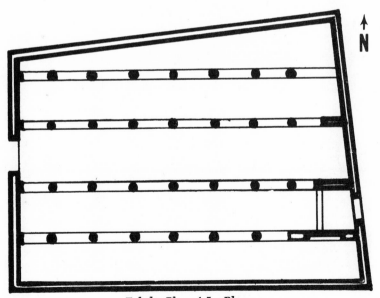

Toledo, Plan of La Blanca

Toledo, La Blanca Prior to Restoration   FOTO MAS

Toledo, Interior of La Blanca   FOTO MAS

In typically medieval style, as the plan shows, no two walls are parallel. The north wall is 81 feet long, whereas the south wall is 87 feet in length. The west wall measures only 59 feet, while the east is over 71 feet. The central nave is almost 39 feet high. There are no balconies. The total effect is powerful and beautiful. The repetitive pattern of the strong columns and arches, the minor repetition of this theme carved in the wall above them between two fine horizontal bands, and the handsome wooden construction above them all lead the eye inevitably to the east wall, the repository for the ark and the law, altogether a most successful design as a synagogue.

The great synagogue of Avila will be discussed in a later section.

Toledo—El Transito

The plan most representative of a beth midrash, that is, the one exhibiting the functions of a house of worship, a house of study, and a house of assembly, each function being well delineated, is to be found in El Tránsito in Toledo. Just a short distance from La Blanca, it too was well removed from the cathedral. It was built by Samuel Abulafia who was, until destroyed by court intrigue in 1360, the treasurer of King Pedro I. There is reason to believe that the synagogue was built in 1357.

Abulafia's synagogue was connected directly to his house, which no longer stands, along the east side of the synagogue. The men of the town and their women both entered from the south, each group having its own entrance. Three other rooms were also along the south. Along the north were three more rooms, obviously used as study rooms for the young and the old. The south room nearest the women's entrance was used as a baptistery when the building became a church; perhaps originally it was a mikveh (ritual bath), or it may have been used to house travelers or students. The rooms adjacent to the men's entrance were either courtrooms used for settling disputes between Jews in accordance with Hebrew law, or they were used for housing transients.

The rectangular prayer hall is about 72 feet long and 29 1/2 feet wide. Its height of just over 37 feet is about the same as the nave of La Blanca, undoubtedly both being restricted by edict and law. The doubled window in the east wall is high above the niche for the ark. On either side of this repository for the Law are the Hebrew dedication tablets. The one on the right reads:

And the house which Samuel built,
And the wooden tower for the reading of the written law,
And its Scrolls of the Law and the crowns thereto,
And its lavers and lamps for lighting,
And its windows like the windows of Ariel.

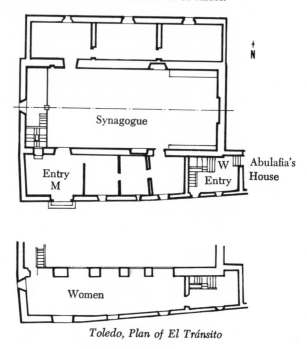

Toledo, Plan of El Tránsito

The inscription on the left translates:

And its courts for them that cherish the perfect law,
And seats, too, for all who sit in the shade of God,
So that those who saw it almost said, "This semblance
Is as the semblance of work which Bezalel wrought."
Go now, ye peoples, and come into my gates
And seek the Lord, for it is a house of God even as Bethel.

(Wischnitzer, p. 34)

Samuel's "wooden tower" refers to the bema, which must have been located in the center of the prayer hall, considering the rather long distance from the ark to the west wall. The "crowns" of the Scrolls of the Law were silver ornaments placed on top of the pro-

Toledo, Exterior of El Tránsito

Toledo, Interior of El Tránsito

jecting wooden rollers, as is the custom in synagogues to this day. The "windows like the windows of Ariel" might be a reference to the Temple (1 Kings 6:4), since "Ariel" is a metaphor for Jerusalem in Isaiah 29:1-2, "Ah, Ariel, Ariel, the city where David is encamped."

The "courts for them that cherish the perfect law" can mean only the use made of some of the ancillary rooms. Abulafia was exceedingly generous in providing "seats, too," since that was not the custom of the day. The reference to Bezalel concerns the artist who made the vessels for the tabernacle of the wilderness (Exodus 31:2 ff). Bethel was mentioned previously in discussing the development of the architectural form of the synagogue, and refers to the place where Jacob had the prophetic vision which caused him to exclaim, "How full of awe is this place; this is no other than the *house of God* (Genesis 28:17).

Other inscriptions glorify Samuel Abulafia in excessive praise, such as "prince among princes of the tribe of Levi." There is also a dedication to King Pedro I, and the name of Rabbi Meir el Levita is found.

The delicately carved frieze between the bands of carved Hebrew lettering shows the same pine-cone motif exhibited in La Blanca and in Segovia. Here and there are to be found the shield of Castile, but woven throughout are Arabic characters which appear to be verses from the Koran, and in at least one place we find the Arabic "La illaha il Allah," which is a most disturbing element in a Jewish house of worship. Probably the carvers' and painters' guild was composed solely of Moors and Arabs who were not supervised too closely, at least in this instance. Abrahams does not list carving or sculpting among fifty-one Spanish-Jewish occupations.

The nicely carved quatrefoil openings in the wooden railing of the women's balcony are identical to the oldest part of the railing in Tudela. The magnificent Mudejar ornamented ceiling rests on brick-bearing walls which were plastered only on the inside. A stone floor completes the construction.

In 1967 the sarcophagus was removed and a tile mosaic was uncovered. Its location indicates that the bema was toward the center of the room and steps led up from side aisles to the ark. The remains show seven candles, a portion of a larger menorah. The colors and design are simple but quite attractive. Undoubtedly the entire floor was originally covered by a tile mosaic.

Toledo, Ceiling of El Tránsito

Toledo, Windows of El Tránsito

Toledo, Detail of El Tránsito

Toledo, Women's Balcony

Toledo, Detail

Toledo, Detail

CORDOBA

The synagogue in Córdoba is of special interest because the first Hebrew religious service in modern Spain was held there in 1935 on the occasion of the 800th anniversary of Maimonides, that truly great Jewish philosopher. At that time the Spanish people erected a statue in his honor in Córdoba and renamed the square in front of it

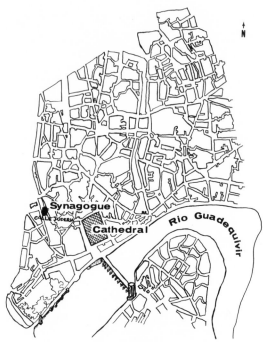

Map of Córdoba

the Plaza Maimonides. The square is a short distance from the Calle Judería which is at the northwest corner of the Great Mosque, now the Cathedral. Leading from the square itself is the Calle de los Judíos, and the synagogue is located in this street.

This one, however, was not the great synagogue of Córdoba. That edifice, built in 1250, was of such a height that it aroused the wrath of the local archdeacon who appealed to the Pope for help. Innocent IV then commanded by apostolic letter "to enforce the authority of your office against the Jews in this regard." Sixty-five years later the existing building was constructed of more modest proportions. Expropriated in 1492, it was converted into a hospital named for Saint Quiteria. In 1588 it became the property of the Brotherhood of Shoemakers and was reconsecrated to Saints Crispin and Crispinian. Declared a national monument in 1885, the building was restored in 1900 under the direction of the architect Mariano Gonzales Rojas. Another restoration was carried out in 1928.

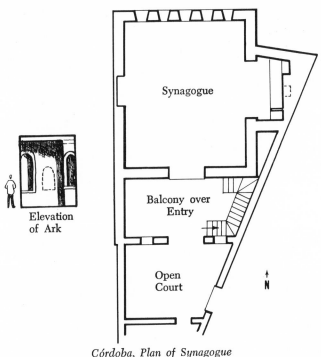

Córdoba, Plan of Synagogue

The round-headed wooden doorway in the street wall leads to an open courtyard measuring 12 feet by 16 feet (average), which leads on the south to an auxiliary building (at present a house) and on the north to an entry hall just 9 1/2 feet deep. Above the entry is the women's gallery. The architect Czekelius believes that the entry and women's balcony were later additions. The prayer hall itself is only 21 feet wide and 23 feet deep, permitting a simple timber hipped roof to be built on the stuccoed brick-bearing walls. Wooden beams angle upward from each corner of the walls, and collar beams a short distance below the ridge serve as supports for a rectangular wooden gridwork used as a flat portion of the ceiling.

The wooden jack rafters tie into the hip beams or the collar beams, as the case may be. The tile roof rests on a wooden deck. The floor is of stone.

Because of the angle of the street it was possible to build the recess for the Scrolls of the Law slightly more than 6 feet deep and over 10 feet wide at its widest point. In addition, at least two niches were provided beyond the recess, the northern one being 25 inches wide and 13 inches deep, and the southern one measuring 17 1/2 inches in width and 22 inches in depth. Traces of a third niche between these two seem to be apparent, but because of its lesser height it was used for some other purpose, if it existed at all. (In 1968 the writer directed the removal of the bricks from this suspect niche, and found that originally there had indeed been a hollowed space in the stone backup wall. The brick wall along the side was also cut open, revealing a room that had not been used for some time.) The ceiling of the entire ark area is much lower than that of the prayer hall. Conceivably there was a curtain near the front of it (the walls of the sanctuary project into that area 9 inches on the north and 4 inches on the south) so that it would be shut off from view when the house of prayer (beth tefillah) was used as a house of assembly (beth knesseth).

On the west wall another recess is found, this one being only 18 inches deep and 5 feet wide. The ornamental arch over it suggests a type of throne; perhaps the seats for the rabbi and the khazzan were located therein, with the bema projecting from it out into the prayer hall. Certainly it is high enough for this purpose, remembering that the bema was a raised platform, often seven or eight steps above the floor, in other places. There is physical evidence on the walls that this bema was raised exactly five steps.

Natural lighting is accomplished by three windows along the south wall above the women's balcony and five single round-headed clerestory windows along the north wall. Both sets obtain light from adjacent courtyards.

The interior plaster was intricately carved in a manner quite reminiscent of El Tránsito, except that Arabic lettering exists only on the west wall. The scale in Córdoba is appropriate to its size and height: there are no boldly projecting pine cones, the bands of lettering are smaller and not carved in such deep relief, and the geometric patterns, while varying from wall to wall and place to place, are lacy, delicate, and repetitive. Over the ark the ornamental rec-

Córdoba, Street of Synagogue

Córdoba, Synagogue Entrance

tangular panel was surrounded by Hebrew lettering and surmounted by a horizontal pattern of 18 small arches. While Mrs. Wischnitzer feels that this was an allusion to the numerical value 18 of the Hebrew word *khai* ("life"), and thus to the Biblical adage that "Torah is life" (Proverbs 4:22), it is much more logical to claim that they refer to the 18 blessings of the Amidah. The Amidah is recited by the pious Jew every day of his life, is contained in every

Córdoba, Western Wall   FOTO MAS

Jewish prayer service, and was written about four hundred years before the Córdoba synagogue was built. Surely the motif of "18" was intended in that direct context, and not something far-fetched.

The Hebrew inscription tablet set in an ornamental panel to the right of the ark translates:

A miniature sanctuary and a house of testimony built by
Issac Moheb son of the honorable Ephraim
In the year 75 as a temporary structure.
Arise, O God, haste to rebuild Jerusalem.

Córdoba, Women's Balcony

Córdoba, Detail of Plaque

The words *mikdash méat* ("miniature sanctuary") indicate that either the sinagoga mayor was still standing or, more likely, that Issac Moheb considered this to be a substitute temple to be used until the true temple was once again built in Jerusalem ("temporary structure"). The "year 75" is an abridgment for the year 5075 of the Hebrew calendar, corresponding to the year 1315 CE. The hole in the wall above the ark could well have held the support for the ner tamid (eternal light).

Near the bema recess on the west wall is found an inscription beginning with the words "Like the tower of David is thy neck." Cantera feels that this passage comes from the Song of Songs 4:4 and alludes to the "tower of wood" used in the Book of Nehemiah 8:4 for the pulpit from which Ezra read the Torah to his people.

One wonders whether or not Moheb built this chapel adjacent to his house, as did Abulafia, but there is no doubt from reading the inscription that Issac was a much more modest man than Samuel.

Former Mosques

The kings of Castile were at times so favorably disposed toward their Jewish subjects that they gave them mosques to be used as synagogues, two of which are still standing in Toledo. The finest remaining example of such transfer is the Bib-al-Mardon mosque, erected in 960 CE. About two hundred years later it was used as a synagogue and still later became the church known today as the Iglesia Cristo de la Luz (Church of Christ of the Light). Its plan shows a rectangular hall with a rounded apse to the east and a separate entry hall and women's section to the west. Nine domes of varied shapes, all derived from the mosque in Córdoba, are supported on four columns with Visigothic capitals. The brick exterior has beautiful three-dimensional patterns, together with carved Arabic lettering in the west wall. The Arabic for *Allah* is still visible, repeated several times. If the building were used as a synagogue for as much as two hundred years, which seems likely, the Jews must have come to feel that it was natural and right for a beth tefillah to have such lettering. After all, two hundred years is about eight generations. One can hardly blame Samuel Abulafia, then, for permitting his craftsmen to carve into his walls "Allah is the only true God," provided they did it in a language he could not read.

The Casa de la Santa Hermandad (the House of the Saintly

Toledo, Mosque "Cristo de la Luz"   FOTO MAS

Toledo, Interior of Mosque   FOTO MAS

Brotherhood), often called the Posada de la Santa Hermandad, is located next to the Cathedral. It is known that at one time there was a Calle de la Sinagoga near the Cathedral. A simple two-story building of irregular shape with interior courtyards used as light wells, the Posada had a Moslem chapel on the first floor at the east end. The Arabs used the open courtyard as their prayer hall, as was their custom. The building has been referred to as a synagogue by Postal and Abramson, but no dates are given. It is known that in 1494 it became the seat of Torquemada's Inquisition, with the tribunal meeting in the large room of the second floor. Judging the

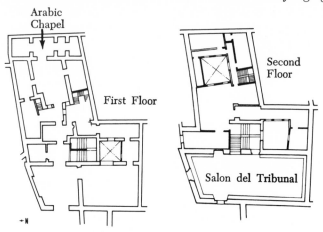

Toledo, Plan of Hermandad

character of Torquemada by that which has been written about him, it seems reasonable that he would elect a former Jewish prayer hall for his courtroom, provided it had not been converted into a church. The balance of this building could well have served the Inquisition as a prison with torture chambers. The room of the tribunal has an unexplained niche in the east wall, which was undoubtedly for the ark of the synagogue. The doorway and window in the east are in accord with the Biblical Daniel's mode of prayer, previously discussed. The greater width than depth would actually have been excellent if the bema were placed along the west wall. The other rooms would have been used by the Jews as study rooms, courtrooms, and hospitality rooms.

9. DISCOVERIES

Let us now consider two cases where the writer believes that he has newly identified former synagogues. The locations are at Paredes de Nava in the province of Palencia in northern Spain and at Avila, capital of the province of the same name in central Spain. The buildings are today Christian churches.

PAREDES DE NAVA

Cantera states that the Jews of Paredes de Nava converted en masse at the time of Vicente Ferrer. There is no written description anywhere of an existing building which was formerly a synagogue in that Spanish town, and yet it seems reasonable to believe that the Iglesia Cristo de la Bella Cruz (Church of Christ of the Beautiful Cross) was a synagogue for perhaps four hundred years before it was consecrated. It is located in the judería on an unpaved street near an unpaved square. Not far away two other churches are being restored.

The plan of Bella Cruz is that of a rectangular hall 84 feet long and 23 1/2 feet wide, with a one-story lean-to on the north having interior dimensions of 15 feet in width and 63 feet in length. There is a small entry porch on the south side. Inside, the westernmost quarter has a wood-floored balcony supported by wooden beams resting on two 8-inch wooden posts.

The tile roof rests on a wooden deck carried by stuccoed brick vaulting in the nearly square bays. Longitudinally semicircular brick arches are 31 inches thick and occur on 20-foot-4-inch centers, there being a clearance of 16 feet 6 inches from the wooden floor to the spring line. The 42-inch-thick brick exterior walls are plastered on the inside face, and the attached brick buttresses which support the arches extend 11 inches into the inside. The few windows are placed high up on the walls. The original building dates from about the year 1000 CE.

The entire effect on the exterior is not unlike the fifth-century synagogue at Umm el-Kanatir, which was located in the Israeli desert. There, too, one finds a small porch with a pitched roof supported by two stone columns, and a few small windows high up on the walls. At Paredes de Nava, though, the entrance was placed at the center of the long side rather than at the end of the building. It is obvious that the eastern quarter of Bella Cruz was added in the fifteenth century: the exterior stone buttresses contrast with the original interior brick buttresses, and the eave design changes from patterned brickwork to carved stone. The quiet little porch is of

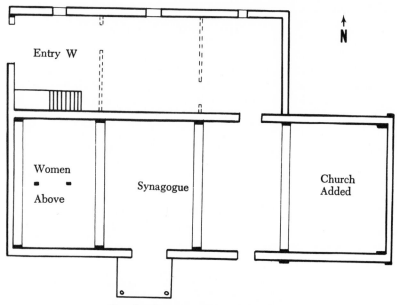

Paredes de Nava, Plan of Synagogue

Mozarabic style; the wooden ceiling joists rest on a carved wooden beam with arched plaster infillings between them. The two stone columns have simple enough bases, but their carved capitals are obviously executed in the shape of the Scrolls of the Law. One sees immediately that the stone "spindles" or "rollers" at the tops of the columns are not Greek or Roman forms nor their derivatives, and are not purely ornamental; they are meant rather to represent the Torah as it is found in the ark, the flat column top representing the parchment on which the Torah is written. The carving in the wooden beam is purely ornamental and has no significance.

Paredes de Nava, Synagogue

Paredes de Nava, Porch Detail

A further strong suggestion as to the original use of this structure is to be found in the balcony. Much of the wood is of the same age as the porch, that is, it predates the year 1400 CE and hence was part of the original edifice. If the building were originally a church, the wooden balcony would be difficult to explain. Even more strange would be the door leading from the balcony to the stairway

Paredes de Nava, Addition

in the room to the north, but if this church were originally a synagogue, the balcony would have been the women's gallery, which is surely what it was.

One may also reasonably speculate that the large room to the north of the prayer hall, which is presently used for storage, was formerly subdivided into three chambers: a women's entry hall and two classrooms which doubled as courtrooms or hospitality rooms. The fenestration suggests that this was so.

In summary, then, the Jews of Paredes de Nava all converted to Catholicism in 1391 or shortly thereafter, and the eastern quarter of the building under discussion was added in the 1400's, perhaps removing and replacing an apse or niche for the ark. The stone capitals of the columns of the porch seem strongly reminiscent of the Scrolls of the Law. The interior balcony was most reasonably used as a women's section, and the northern room was probably subdivided into three rooms, each about 15 feet by 21 feet. The evidence appears conclusive that the present Iglesia Cristo de la Bella Cruz was originally a synagogue, with the ark at its east end and the bema in the center of the prayer hall.

AVILA

The first recorded evidence of Jews in Avila concerns one David Centen in the year 1085. By 1291 the Jewish people of Avila were numerous enough to pay 74,000 maravedis in taxes, and they possessed several synagogues. Professor Francisco Cantera, the director of the Institute of Hebrew and Near Eastern Studies in Madrid, feels that the judería was confined to the northeast quadrant of the city, within the walls which are still standing, and was entered through both the Mariscal and the San Vicente gates. The present-day Spanish historian Pilar León Tello states: "In the thirteenth century Jews lived in the Plaza de Santo Tomé, Barrio de Cesteros, in the Barrio de San Gil, Calle de Estrada, and in other parts of the city. But the most typical Jewish area, principally in the fourteenth century, was the Yuradero, adjacent to the Church of San Vicente."[1] The Yuradero quarter is the area described by Cantera. However, in 1480 the cortes of Toledo required that Jews and Moors thenceforth live in special barrios, gathering there within two years. On April 24, 1481, Rodrigo Alvárez Maldonado was commissioned to execute this law in Segovia and Avila, and the Jews were moved outside the walls to an area in the southwest. After Juce Franco, his father, and his brothers were burned at the stake in Avila on November 16, 1491, for religious reasons, there was a great uprising. The Jews were massacred and plundered, leading to a special edict by the Crown which took them under royal protection.

It is difficult to estimate the number of Jews in Avila, since there was no census taken before 1530.[2] According to León Tello, it is possible that the major part of the population of Avila were Jews. She estimates that 3,000 went into exile in 1492.

1. *Judíos de Avila*, p. 9.   2. *Ibid.*, p. 30.

Surely there must have been more than the one synagogue on Calle Lomo in the Yuradero that is mentioned by Cantera in *Sinagogas españolas*. In fact, León Tello writes: "They increased the number of synagogues in the mid 1400's. . . . Other synagogues were in the Calle Andrín near the judería, and near it there is cited in a document of 1417 the synagogue of Moçon. There was still another

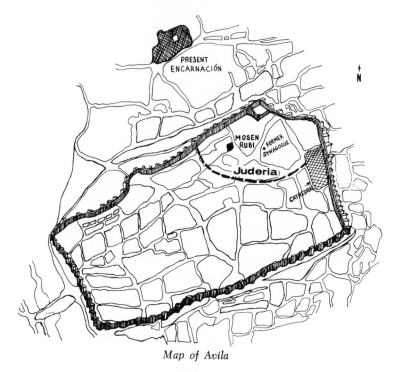

Map of Avila

named the Ben Forad, or Bilforado, that was established in the quarter of the Cobaleda near the monastery of Santa María del Carmen. The one synagogue that one cannot localize is mentioned in a book of anniversaries of the Cathedral in 1460, established by Don Symuel in the house where Gonzalo González lived alone."[3] In a footnote she says that this one may have been in the house whose present address is 2 Calle del Pocillo. After the Jews left Spain, two of the synagogues in Avila were sold at auction to the canon Francisco de Avila, "one of these in the old judería, the other 'near the

3. *Ibid.*, p. 28.

gate of La Malaventura,' perhaps constructed after the pact of the cortes concerning the separation" (that is, the law of 1480).[4] In this last statement she seems to be in error: although the cited law did not affect those synagogues that were in existence, it did prohibit the building of new ones. However, it may have been built then, even so.

Neither of the two purchased by de Avila was the one referred to by Cantera, for in the archives of the monastery Encarnación of Avila we find that Bishop Alonso de Fonseca on July 8, 1485, converted that synagogue into the Church of All Saints.[5] Its ruins were uncovered in 1968 when repairs were being made on the Church of Encarnación, and except for Miss León Tello's speculations concerning house number 2 on Calle del Pocillo, no trace remains of any of the synagogues that have been mentioned.

However, there is a great deal of architectural and other evidence that the present Chapel of Mosen Rubi in Avila was originally built in 1462 as a great synagogue. The Chapel is located on the Plaza Mosen Rubi at the intersection of Calle Bracamonte and Calle de López Núñez; the former street leads to the Mariscal Gate, and the latter passes under the Puerta de San Vicente. Thus, the structure was built within the confines of the old judería. There is now attached to it a lovely Renaissance wing which is at present attached to a convent.

The name *Mosen Rubi* stems from Mosen Rubi de Bracamonte, or Rubin de Braquemonte, an "almirante" of France.[6] It seems that in 1396 a French gentleman named Mosen Manriga sold to Mosen Rubi de Bracamonte certain property (13 "doblas") that he had obtained from the king. That particular year is of great interest, for it coincides with the year that the Jews were expelled from France, and leads one to believe that Braquemonte was a French Jew. Mosen Rubi married Inez de Mendoza, the daughter of Pedro González de Mendoza, and she bore him a son, Mosen Juan, and a daughter Juana. There were three other daughters: Isabel; María,

---

4. *Ibid.*

5. According to Ballesteros, *Estudio histórico de Avila*, p. 183.

6. The family history delineated here has been taken from several manuscripts in the National Library at Madrid and in the Royal Archives at Simancas. The title *mosen* was apparently from the French *monsieur*. The title *almirante* may have had in those days a meaning different from *admiral*. In fact it seems to have been a hereditary title, since Rubi's son Juan was also an almirante of France.

who married Pedro de Avila; and Leonor, who married Fernando de Albarado. The son Juan inherited from Mosen Rubi, and just before he died in 1423 sold all his property to his sister Juana. Ten years later Juana married the illustrious Albaro de Avila, a courtier of both the king of Aragon and his son and majordomo to the infante. It would seem that Juan sold the property to his sister to avoid splitting it into several parts by multiple inheritance. Albaro and Juana had two daughters and three sons: Diego de Valencia, Albaro de Bracamonte, and Pedro de Sujan who married María de Mendoza.

The total estate of Juana and her husband was a large one. It involved the villages of Medina de Rioseco, Fuentelsol, Peñada, "and others," the 15,000-marcos rents of the butcher shops in the city of Avila, and the 10,000-marcos rents of "certain places" of the sector of Cobaleda which was located at "the end of the city." These were large sums of money, for Rabbis Yucef and Meir received as salary only 500 marcos a year in Avila from 1460 to 1465.

Juana de Bracamonte outlived her husband Albaro de Avila and all of her sons, and the estate was inherited by the daughter who had married a de Herrera. (It is known that Diego Martínez de Herrera was a Jew who converted to Catholicism.) Their daughter María de Herrera married her uncle Andrés Vásquez and subsequently inherited the family fortune. On October 2, 1512, she wrote her will and by one of its clauses established a hospital for the poor, to be named Anunciación de Nuestra Señora. This hospital was later taken over by the convent which is presently attached to the Chapel of Mosen Rubi.[7]

María's will further ordained that a church be built for the hospital. Now we come to the crux of the matter. The question before us is whether the Chapel of Mosen Rubi was built as a Catholic church in fulfillment of María's will, or whether it was built earlier, before the will, as a synagogue and was later converted into a church. The writer contends that the latter proposition is the correct one and will now adduce the evidence.

María de Herrera stipulated that the hospital she endowed should have a capacity of thirteen patients, with servants, a doctor, an apothecary, and six chaplains, altogether not over twenty-five persons. The chapel would have been built in ratio to such an at-

7. The convent started as a college for girls in 1480 in Aldeanueva de Santa Cruz, and became a religious convent school in 1522.

tendance, and not the size of Capilla Mosen Rubi which can easily hold sixteen times that number. Furthermore, María willed that the chapel be built of "good materials, without paint," except that all the interior wood was to be painted white. Now in the Chapel of Mosen Rubi wood is almost nonexistent: the walls, floor, and ceiling are of expensive stone, so expensive that the chapel is completely illogical as a part of a poorhouse. It is much more logical to suppose

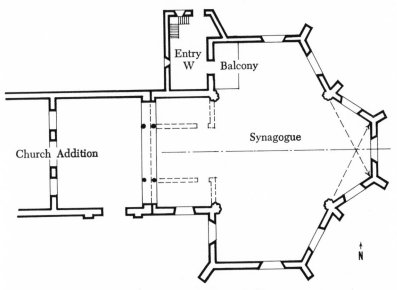

Avila, Plan of Mosen Rubi

that the executor of María's will, her nephew Diego de Bracamonte, built a wooden hospital and living quarters for the chaplains, etc., adjacent to an existing church (that is, a synagogue recently converted into a church). It is known that María's hospital burned down and was later rebuilt; there is architectural evidence to corroborate these facts.

In summary, the Chapel of Mosen Rubi is much too large and too expensive to have been built as a church for the devotions of a very small, very poor congregation, and it is not built of the materials prescribed in María de Herrera's will.

Can we date the building of the structure that is now the chapel? High up on the interior eastern wall the date 1521 is carved in Roman characters, but it is spread out over several stones instead of being carved into one. Had the date been incised originally, it would surely have been in just one block, and one must conclude that it was chiseled long after the building was completed, that is, when the former synagogue was consecrated as a Catholic church.

But the date of the construction of the chapel may be learned from another marker. There is a stone plaque mounted high up on the interior of what was the western wall of the original building. In Roman lettering it reads:

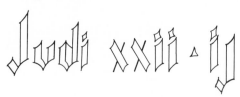

that is, *Judi 22-24*. If this is interpreted to refer to the Epistle of Saint Jude, verses 22 through 24 when taken out of context can hardly apply to this structure; besides, the three lines form an incomplete verse. It is much more logical to translate the inscription as "of the Jews 22-24," meaning that the building was constructed in the Jewish years 22-24, that is, the years 5222 to 5224 in the Hebrew calendar, in a manner similar to the inscription in Córdoba. The Hebrew year 5222 corresponds to the year 1462 of the Common Era. The architectural style of the chapel is more in accord with that of this earlier date than with that of the later.

In 1462 Mosen Rubi de Bracamonte's daughter Juana, who had married Albaro de Avila, would have been a little over sixty years old. It is certain that she lived to an old age, for she outlived her three sons. She was quite wealthy and could certainly afford to build a splendid synagogue across the street from her house. The Bracamonte mansion is near the chapel, next to the Mariscal Gate, within the old judería, and the Avila palace is next to it. Certainly a man as rich and powerful as Albaro de Avila would not have lived within the typically Jewish section of the city unless he were himself a Jew.[8] The fact that he held an important position in court, as did his father Sancho (who in fact proclaimed Henry IV as Prince of Asturias), does not prove that he was not Jewish. Samuel Levi, the builder of a synagogue in Toledo, was the treasurer of King

8. The name *Avila* was quite commonly Jewish, and still is today, perhaps because Avila was the center of Cabala. The mystic Mosé de León was born in Avila province and organized the *Zohar*, the "bible" of Cabala.

Avila, Mosen Rubi, View Looking Northeast

Avila, Interior Looking West

Pedro. Had Juana in fact built a synagogue she would have done so in honor of her father Mosen Rubi, as was a Jewish custom.

The carved stone plaques on the buttresses of the Chapel of Mosen Rubi contain the coats of arms of the Bracamonte, Avila, and Herrera families. These are now easily explained. The work on the building was started by Juana, a Bracamonte married to an Avila, and completed by her daughter, married to a Herrera. It was quite common to honor the donor family, as was done in the carved plaster in Toledo, by sculpting the family crest into the building, and since no human figures were carved, the action is in accord with Jewish law.

There is the question of obtaining permission in 1462 to build a new synagogue. Law number 109 of King Henry IV of Castile prohibited synagogue construction, but it was promulgated on January 16, 1465, one year after the completion of Mosen Rubi. Still, even in 1462 permission to build a new synagogue would certainly not have been given if another were already in use. Yet Cantera's synagogue on Calle Lomo was a church *no later* than 1476. It is reasonable to believe that it was in the time of Vicente Ferrer, *circa* 1391, that the Calle Lomo synagogue was consecrated a church by the Catholics. At that time, unless they had been looted, set on fire, and destroyed, it was only a fitting sequel, to paraphrase the words of Innocent III, that "places divested of the blind Jewish perversion of faith should receive the light of grace under the name of the Christian religion." Hence we can assume that the Jews were given permission to erect a synagogue in 1462, and more particularly that Juana de Bracamonte de Avila was the chief donor. Note that 1462 was almost fifty years after Pope Benedict interdicted synagogue construction, and that the year was an amicable time for the Jews. Henry IV lived on until December 18, 1474, and when he died there was great mourning by the Jews. Evidently he had been good to them, and this is witnessed by the fact that many synagogues were built during his reign. Perhaps he was influenced by his Jewish friends and courtiers, the Avilas.

The plan of the original building lends support to the proposition that Mosen Rubi was first a synagogue. Certainly not a rectangle and hardly a cruciform, the large hall would have been ideally suited for Hebrew worship. With the ark in the apse on the east, the bema in the center of the room, and seats facing either north or south, every one of the congregants could have seen the ark and the

Avila, Mosen Rubi, View Looking Southwest

Avila, Interior Looking East

bema without turning. It is even possible that in this one instance the bema was located adjacent to the ark, with all seats facing east. A plan exhibiting angled walls, such as this one, had been used as a synagogue, and therefore as a church, approximately at the time of Christ, but was not in use in the Middle Ages.

The prototype of the plan emphasizing width against length can be seen in Babylonian temples. Furthermore, since this building was used as a chapel and not as a cathedral, there would be no choir during Christian services, and it would actually have been wrong to have the east wall of the apse in full view of all the worshipers. In addition, the room on the northwest corner can hardly be construed to have been built as a small chapel or a baptistery; it is more logical to contend that it was originally the women's entrance, the stairway therein leading to the women's balcony, which is now the organ loft.

Finally, it can be demonstrated that even the quasi-cruciform shape of the plan was destroyed by rooms flanking the westerly entrance hall, rooms that are no longer in existence. Consider the photograph of the interior looking westward. Above the columns there is a seemingly unnecessary stone arch set within the stone wall—the coursing of the wall below the arch does not match adjacent coursing. Furthermore, there is a certain awkwardness in the arrangement just above the columns where the horizontal line of the head of the round arches abuts an elliptical rosette. It would seem that the round arches originally contained windows identical to those high up on the walls; the size of the openings is the same. The doubled columns replaced walls at the main entrance. That these walls continued back toward the prayer hall is evidenced by the former window (or was it a door?) on the south wall in what is now a niche at ground level. The view of the exterior looking northeast shows that the niche at the right of the present entrance has a much deeper reveal than the other two. Thus it is established that there were two rooms flanking the original entry hall, one used as a courtroom and the other as a study room. Following the 18-foot-6-inch module of the entire floor plan, each of these rooms was 9 feet 3 inches by 18 feet 6 inches.

The most conclusive proof of all, though, is found on close inspection of the view of the exterior looking toward the northeast. Just under the roof on the wall behind what was the women's balcony the photograph unmistakably shows a carved *six-pointed star*!

Avila, Detail of Buttress

Avila, Former Window

There is no doubt that the Chapel of Mosen Rubi was constructed as a great synagogue in 1462, perhaps the last such built before the Jews left Spain thirty years later.

It is certainly a handsome building, with its interior completely of stone—floor, walls, and ceiling. The stone ceiling panels are carried on stone ribs in the Gothic manner. The tile roof rests on the stone ceiling. The great interior height of over 60 feet is matched by no other existing synagogue on the entire Iberian Peninsula. Excluding the buttresses and the women's entry, the outside width and length are both approximately 80 feet. The prayer hall had room for well over three hundred seats, in addition to those in the women's section. The sheer beauty of its dignity, simplicity, and classic restraint in the use of symbolism and ornamentation could well serve as a model for today.

10. CONCLUSION

Until 1492 Jews had resided on the Iberian Peninsula for over 2,000 years, more or less continuously. Some arrived with the Phoenicians, many more came with the Romans, some as slaves, others as traders or farmer immigrants. At times life was pleasant, at times harsh for the Hebrews, there being no fixed or consistent policy with either the Christian or the Moslem rulers. In fact, had it not been for the ill-advised "purity of the blood" ideology adopted by the Spaniards about 1480, it is reasonable to believe that neither Jews nor Moors would have been exiled twelve years later.

The religious buildings of the Jews fall into two categories, the ordinary synagogue and the great synagogue. The latter, in a manner analogous to a cathedral, was built in centers of Judaism where usually several of the former type existed. In both instances they were restricted in size and in height by a jealous Church which exerted influence on the secular rulers. Hence with a seating capacity of only about four hundred, the great synagogues were not vast, but were certainly impressive. The three which remain intact are to be found in Segovia, Toledo (La Blanca), and Avila. The Iglesia Mosen Rubi in Avila has never as yet been identified as having originally been Jewish, but the evidence is overwhelming. The ordinary synagogues were much less formal and had attached to them several ancillary rooms for study, for Hebrew legal procedures, and perhaps for lodging rooms for travelers or students. The great synagogue had at most one or two such rooms.

The entrance for the men was usually through a walled courtyard, reminiscent of the Jerusalem Temple, or through a porch which had a gossip bench. After the ninth or tenth century women had a separate entrance and were seated separately, usually in a wooden balcony which had a carved wood railing. The ark, which contained the Scrolls of the Law, became fixed in position on the eastern (Jerusalem-oriented) wall. The reader of the Law, who became the explainer and teacher (rabbi), stood on a raised wooden platform in the center of the prayer hall or along its western wall. These several items constituted the sole plan requirements of the beth tefillah (house of prayer).

The construction system generally incorporated thick brick-bearing walls plastered on their interiors. Two wealthy donors had the plaster ornately carved, at Córdoba¹and at Toledo (El Tránsito). The great synagogues of Segovia and Toledo (La Blanca) also have some carving. Usually though, the stucco was left smooth and plain; it may have originally been painted with an ornamental geometric design, as was the wood in Tudela (the plaster in Tudela was carved in a simple repetitive geometric pattern), or it may have been adorned with passages in Hebrew, as seen today in Lisbon and throughout Italy and Israel. Centuries of whitewash obliterated what was painted, if anything.

The universal tile roof was carried on wood construction spanning transversely from wall to wall. Where the span was considered too large the wood was run longitudinally, carried by brick walls over brick arch openings adjoining interior buttressing. In Paredes de Nava plastered vaults were used instead of longitudinal wood beams. In two instances four interior stone columns were employed, at Tomar and at Cáceres. At Tomar the roof is carried on vaults, whereas at Cáceres the columns support a series of transverse brick arches carrying stuccoed brick walls. The synagogue at Paredes, incidentally, is another one which has never as yet been so identified. Only at Avila do we find buttressed stone walls supporting a ceiling of ribbed stone panel vaults in a fine Gothic manner.

Fenestration was always accomplished by means of clear glass, usually set in high openings to obtain privacy. The size of the windows varied from place to place, but generally a window was roundheaded and contained two roundheaded panes with a single mullion, representing the Ten Commandments. Another favorite design motif was the theme of five, recalling the Torah (the five books of Moses). Thus, there is often found five windows in a wall, or five openings in a series of arches, as at Segovia and Cáceres.

Floors were of wood, brick, or stone, depending on the wealth of the donors. Jews never taxed themselves for construction. While many synagogues were built by individuals or by individual families, some were erected by Jewish societies, and others by voluntary contributions from the community as a whole.

In modern times the Jews of Lisbon received official permission to build a synagogue in 1902. A generation later Sir Alec Kaduri built one for the Jews of Pórto, and now with a new constitution guaranteeing freedom of religion, once again magnificent structures for Hebrew worship will be erected in Spain, after a hiatus of five hundred years.

Lisbon, Present Synagogue

Lisbon, Interior of Present Synagogue

BIBLIOGRAPHY

Abrahams, I. *Jewish Life in the Middle Ages.* Cleveland: World Publishing Co., 1961 (first published 1896).

Asher, A. *The Itinerary of R. Benjamin of Tudela.* London, 1840.

Ballesteros, E. *Estudio histórico de Avila.* Avila, 1896.

Barnett, R. *The Synagogue of Bevis Marks.* Oxford: Oxford University Press, 1960.

Baron, S. *The Jewish Community,* vol. 6. Philadelphia: Jewish Publication Society of America, 1942.

Calvert, A. *Spain,* 2 vols. New York: William Helburn, 1924.

————. *Valladolid.* New York: John Lane Co., 1908.

————, and W. Gallichan. *Cordova.* New York: John Lane Co., 1907.

Cantera Burgos, F. *Sinagogas españolas.* Madrid: Arias Montano, 1955.

Caro Boroja, J. *Los Judíos en la España.* Madrid.

Carramolino, J. *Historia de Avila.* Madrid, 1872.

Czekelius, O. "Antiguas sinagogas de España," *Arquitectura,* vol. 13 (October, 1931).

García Bellido, A. Article in *Sefarad* (Madrid), vol. 22.

Gómez-Moreno, M. *A Visit to the Synagogue of the Transito.* Madrid: Fundaciones Vega, 1966.

Goodenough, E. *Jewish Symbols in the Greco-Roman Period,* 4 vols. New York: Pantheon Books, 1953.

Holisher, D. *The Synagogue and Its People.* New York: Abelard-Schuman, 1955.

Kampf, A. *Contemporary Synagogue Art.* New York: Union of American Hebrew Congregations, 1966.

Kayserling, M. *Christopher Columbus.* New York: Longmans Green & Co., 1894.

Krautheïmer, R. *Mittelalterliche Synagogen.* Berlin: Frankfurter Verlags-Anstalt, 1927.

Landsberger, F. *A History of Jewish Art.* Cincinnati: Union of American Hebrew Congregations, 1946.

León Tello, P. *Judíos de Avila.* Avila, 1963.

Levy, I. *The Synagogue: Its History and Function.* London: Valentine Mitchell, 1966.

Lindo, E. *The Jews of Spain and Portugal.* London: Longmans Brown, 1898.

Loukomski, G. *Jewish Art in European Synagogues.* London: Longmans Brown, 1898.

Mann, S. "Ancient Synagogues of the Galilee," *Hadassah* Magazine, vol. 47 (April, 1966).

Marcus, J. *The Jew in the Medieval World.* Cleveland: World Publishing Co., 1960.

Mayer, A. *Old Spain.* New York: Brentano, 1921.

Mayoral Fernández, J. *El Municipio de Avila.* Avila, n.d.

Morris, J., and E. Hofer. *The Presence of Spain.* New York: Harcourt, Brace & World, 1964.

Museo de la Santa Hermandad. Toledo: Dirección General de las Bellas Artes, 1958.

Neumark, A. *The Jews in Spain,* vol. 2. Philadelphia: Jewish Publication Society of America, 1944.

Pinkerfield, J. *Bethi HaKnesseth B'Eretz Israel.* Jerusalem: Central Press, 1956.

————. *Bethi Knesseth B'Italia.* Jerusalem: Goldberg's Press, 1954.

Postal, P., and S. Abramson. *The Landmarks of a People.* New York: Hill & Wang, 1962.

Prestel, M. *Die Baugeschichte des jüdischen Heiligtums.* Strasbourg, 1902.

Puerta Vizcaino, J. de la. *La Sinagoga Balear.* Palma de Mallorca: Editorial Clumba, 1951.

Quiros, T. de. *The Spanish Jews.* Madrid: Rivadeneyra S.A., 1966.

Rodríquez Almeida, E. *Avila.* Madrid, 1961.

Rosenau, H. *A Short History of Jewish Art.* London: Clarke & Co., 1948.

Santos Simões, J. *Tomar e a sua Judaria.* Tomar: Museu Luso-Hebraico, 1943.

Tachau, W. *The Architecture of the Synagogue.* American Jewish Yearbook, 1926.

Vaca de Osma, J. *Avila.* Madrid: Publicaciones Españolas, 1964.

Viegas Guerreiro, M. *Os Judeus na História de Portugal.* Lisbon, 1965.

Volavkova, H. *The Synagogue Treasures.* Prague: Sfinx, 1949.

Wischnitzer, R. *The Architecture of the European Synagogue.* Philadelphia: Jewish Publication Society of America, 1964.

————. *The Paintings of the Dura Synagogue.* Chicago: University of Chicago Press, 1948.

Zeitlin, S. *Proceedings.* New York: American Academy of Jewish Research, 1930.

UNIVERSITY OF FLORIDA MONOGRAPHS

Social Sciences